THE ECONOMICS OF THE DEVELOPING COUNTRIES

The Economics of the Developing Countries

H. MYINT

Senior Lecturer in the Economics of Underdeveloped Countries in the University of Oxford

HUTCHINSON OF LONDON

HUTCHINSON & CO. (*Publishers*) LTD
178–202 Great Portland Street, London, W.1

London Melbourne Sydney
Auckland Bombay Toronto
Johannesburg New York

★

First published 1964
Reprinted 1964
Reprinted 1965

This book has been set in Times New Roman,
printed in Great Britain on Smooth Wove paper
by The Anchor Press, Ltd., and bound by Wm.
Brendon & Son Ltd., both of Tiptree, Essex.

Contents

5

I

Introduction:
The Post-war Approach to
the Underdeveloped Countries

There are two main driving forces behind the study of the underdeveloped countries. The first, which has grown rapidly under the pressure of post-war international tensions, is concerned with the need to do something urgently about the problem of poverty in these countries. The second, which has a longer academic tradition, is concerned with trying to understand the reasons for the great differences in economic development between the underdeveloped and the developed countries; it is concerned with the nature and causes of the 'Poverty of Nations'. Current ideas of the underdeveloped countries can best be understood against the background of these two approaches and their interaction upon each other.

The first line of approach starts with the broad fact that a small group of countries in North America, Western Europe and Australia and New Zealand enjoy per capita national incomes of $1,000 a year or more, while a large group of countries in most of Asia, Africa and Latin America (with over half the world population between them) have typical per capita incomes of $100 or less[1]. It stresses this vast gap in

1. *Per capita National Product of Fifty-five countries: 1952-4*, United Nations Statistical Papers, Series E, no. 4, 1957.

incomes between the rich and the poor countries of the world, and it urges the rich to increase its help to the poor.

The per capita income definition of the underdeveloped countries undoubtedly succeeds in focussing attention on the poverty of the countries. Differences in per capita money incomes are only an approximate measure of differences in per capita real incomes and standards of living. But the gap in the per capita money incomes between the developed and the underdeveloped countries is so large that it will not be appreciably affected by taking into account various possible qualifications.

Apart from its primary purpose of publicizing the poverty of the underdeveloped countries, the per capita income definition has somewhat limited uses. To begin with, owing to imperfections in basic statistics in calculating both the total national income and the total population, the per capita income figures for many underdeveloped countries are still very crude and liable to wide margins of error. A difference in per capita incomes of, say, $100 between one underdeveloped country and another may or may not mean very much. Nor would ranking the underdeveloped countries in descending order of their per capita income figures give a reliable gradation of their different levels of poverty.[1] Low income per capita, too, however important, is only one aspect of the complex problem of underdevelopment, and a definition of the underdeveloped countries relying solely on the per capita income criterion is bound to be arbitrary. Thus, if we use the per capita income of $100 as the basis of our definition, we shall be excluding many countries with incomes of up to $400 which are otherwise regarded as underdeveloped. If, on the other hand, we raise

1. For instance, it has been estimated that Burma's per capita income of $50, one of the lowest in the United Nations Table, understates her real income by as much as 300% (cf. C. P. Kindleberger, *Economic Development*, p. 3).

our demarcation line to $400, we shall be including some countries, like Japan, which in spite of having relatively low per capita incomes are 'developed' in other respects (not to speak of a special case like Argentina with an income level above $400 but by no means a 'developed' country).

When we turn to the second line of approach to the under-developed countries there is a definite shift in the focus of attention from the *level* to the *rate of growth* of per capita incomes in these countries. Logically, the fact that the under-developed countries have lower income levels does not neces-sarily mean that they also have a lower rate of growth in incomes than the developed countries. Part of the difference in incomes may simply be due to a later start. But most of the current theories of the underdeveloped countries depict them with stagnant or declining per capita incomes; or, at best, with much slower rates of growth than the developed countries.

This view has gained wide acceptance for at least three reasons. (i) It accords with the popular notion of the under-developed country as a closed traditional society stagnating in primitive isolation. (ii) It gains powerful support from the classical theory of the stationary state brought about by the Malthusian population pressure on land. (iii) It is in tune with the prevailing post-war mood of pessimism and desperation in which 'vicious circles' (of poverty and low wages leading to low investment, and low productivity of labour leading to poverty) loom large in the economists' vision. It has therefore become a part of the 'new orthodoxy' to say that the under-developed countries are held down very firmly by a circular constellation of forces to their 'low-income equilibrium' from which they can be jerked only by a concentrated large-scale development effort; by a 'big push' of heroic dimensions.

How far is this view supported by the record of the economic performance of the underdeveloped countries? Leaving aside

the earlier phases of their history, we may consider their economic performance in the post-war period for which more
statistical information is available from various United Nations
publications.[1] Now these statistics suffer from defects similar
to those which we have noted in the calculation of the per
capita income levels of the underdeveloped countries. When
comparing the real incomes of different underdeveloped
countries one important source of error arises from their widely
varying degrees of inflation and import control, so that com-
parisons made on the basis of the fixed official rates of exchange
do not give a true comparison of the purchasing powers of
national currency units within their respective countries. When
estimating the rate of growth in real income of a given underdeveloped country from the rate of growth in its money income
over a period of time, an analogous source of error arises from
the changes in the purchasing power of money during that
period, which in some cases may be very large, owing to rapid
inflation. I have suggested that a difference in per capita income
of, say, $100 between two underdeveloped countries may or
may not mean very much in real terms. In estimating the rate
of growth also, a similar margin of error must be allowed: an
estimated rate of growth in per capita income below 1% for a
period shorter than three years may or may not mean very
much.

With these reservations, the general picture of the underdeveloped countries' economic performance does not seem to
be one of unmixed gloom. In spite of having the world's highest
rate of population growth, the Latin American region as a
whole (with one or two notable exceptions) seems to be enjoying rates of growth in per capita incomes which compare
favourably with the developed countries. Asia (excluding
Japan) seems to have slower rates of growth (again with one or

1. *World Economic Survey, 1959*, p. 73; *Economic Bulletin for Latin
America*, vol. IV, no. 2, 1959.

two notable exceptions). Information about African rates of growth is still difficult to obtain.

Particular countries, like Indonesia or Argentina, are suffering from a stagnation or a decline in per capita incomes. In many cases population pressure is probably the most important factor but it need not be the only factor; Argentina, for instance, is not overpopulated. Then there is the general run of underdeveloped countries which seem to be enjoying some measure of economic growth though in many cases their growth rates are perhaps too small to be significant in view of the crudity of the estimates. Few of them, however, are stationary in the sense of having both stationary total income and total population; their total income is expanding, but not much more than their population growth. Finally, there are a number of countries like the Philippines or many of the Latin American countries like Mexico or Brazil which have had growth rates of 4% to 5% or even more for periods as long as a decade or so.

This is not altogether surprising because on a closer look the underdeveloped countries, far from being a homogeneous group, are a very mixed bag.

Some (like those in Asia except South-East Asia) suffer from a heavy population pressure on their natural resources in the true Malthusian manner, while others (like those in Latin America) still have abundant natural resources and sparse populations. Some have been opened up for many decades to outside economic and cultural influences, to foreign trade and investment, to the exchange economy, to Hollywood films, while others approximate to the popular notion of the closed traditional society. (Here the difference is perhaps greater between the big towns and the remoter rural districts within each underdeveloped country than between different underdeveloped countries.) Last but not least, some countries have achieved a reasonable degree of law and order, political stability, honest and efficient public administration, which others lack in varying degrees; while many newly independent countries have their ability to create it still untried.

Thus, the first thing to bear in mind about the underdeveloped countries is that beyond the broad common fact of poverty it is rarely safe to make generalizations about them without carefully specifying the *type* of underdeveloped country one is considering. The widely accepted generalization that the underdeveloped countries suffer from little or no rate of growth in their per capita incomes may be true, particularly for the overpopulated type of country. We may even regard this as the most important type in the sense that it embraces the largest number of individuals in the whole of the underdeveloped world. But on the other hand we must carefully guard against trying to apply theories and policies that are appropriate for the overpopulated countries uncritically to other types of country not yet suffering from serious population pressure. By other criteria, such as geographical area or the number of countries involved, these less well-known types of country are just as important. Instead of a monolithic theory to cover all the underdeveloped countries it will be more fruitful to look for alternative theoretical models to suit different types of underdeveloped country.

If at least some underdeveloped countries are not stagnant and may have rates of growth equal to or higher than those normal for the developed countries, what then is the real distinction between them? In this connection I shall briefly touch upon the theory of the 'take-off' associated with the name of Professor W. W. Rostow.[1] According to this theory, the essential difference between the developed and the underdeveloped countries lies not so much in the highness and lowness of their rates of economic growth as in the fact that, while the developed countries can rely on their growth to continue steadily into the future as an automatic and self-generating process, the

1. W. W. Rostow, 'The Take-off into Self-sustained Growth', *Economic Journal*, March 1956.

underdeveloped countries can not. This is because the developed countries have already passed through a phase of intense economic development, the 'take-off', during which the self-generating growth mechanism has been built into their economic structure. In contrast, the economic growth of the underdeveloped countries, even when it is very rapid, is likely to be temporary and sporadic, coming to a stop when the initial stimulus has played itself out. For example, an underdeveloped economy growing rapidly owing to the expansion of a primary export product will sooner or later come to a stop, either because all its natural resources suitable for the production of that export have been brought into use, or because the world market demand for its export ceases to expand. In other words, its growth will be brought to a stop either by diminishing returns or by its inability to switch to new types of economic activity.

Professor Rostow has characterized the take-off by, among other things, a high rate of saving and investment; not less than 10% of national income. Rightly or wrongly, many writers have used this as the basis for the generalization that to promote economic development, the underdeveloped countries must raise their rate of saving and investment above 10% of their national income. The argument for launching on an intense development effort has now broadened somewhat. Before, it was used with special reference to the stagnant underdeveloped countries, to jerk them out of the grip of the 'low-income equilibrium'. Now, all underdeveloped countries, whatever their present rate of growth, should make an intense development effort to achieve the necessary economic momentum for the take-off.

Without entering at this stage into the assumptions behind the advice to save and invest more than 10% of national income, it is worth noting that a country's rate of economic growth depends not only on how much it can save, but also on how productively it can invest this saving. Some underdeveloped countries with a high ratio of export to national income may not find it too difficult to raise their rate of saving by means of marketing boards and other forms of taxation on foreign trade, particularly during export booms. Yet their subsequent rate of growth may still be slow while others seem to be growing more rapidly on a lower rate of saving. What then decides how far a given underdeveloped country is ready to absorb a high rate of saving of over 10% of its national income into productive investment, and to keep on generating this rate of saving and absorbing it into investment? This seems to depend on a complex of less easily measurable qualitative factors such as the skills and attitudes of its people, or the efficiency and flexibility of its economic organization, which Professor Rostow has described as a 'political, social and institutional framework which exploits the impulses to expansion'. Further, according to him, the developed countries had a 'long period' of a century or more to build up these 'preconditions for the take-off'.

Here we come up against the real snags of trying to apply the take-off theory to the underdeveloped countries. Looking back with the wisdom of hindsight on the history of an already developed country, we may be able to say that it took off during a certain period and that therefore such and such a long period before it took off may be regarded as the 'pre-take-off' period. But if we are in the middle of this whole process, as the underdeveloped countries are, it is very difficult to decide where exactly a given underdeveloped country is in this sequence of periods. While the theory gives a clear enough distinction between the take-off and the pre-take-off periods, it does not help us to distinguish between the different sub-stages of the pre-take-off period such as those which lie between the more advanced underdeveloped countries like India or Mexico and the more backward underdeveloped countries which have not even succeeded in maintaining basic law and order and may have to struggle hard merely to survive as separate political units. In particular, the take-off theory does not help us to find out beforehand how ready a given underdeveloped country is for the final take-off phase.

In so far as the underdeveloped countries place themselves somewhere in the middle of the pre-take-off period, they would find Professor Rostow's estimate of the period required to establish the 'preconditions' for the take-off impossibly long and would like to find ways and means of compressing it into a few decades. The engineering problems of building the runway are different from those of becoming airborne and there is no reason to suppose that the same type of economic policy will be equally effective both in trying to establish the preconditions quickly and in assisting the take-off after these preconditions have been established. Here, although there is much discussion about providing the underdeveloped countries with the material 'infrastructure' such as transport systems and power stations, there has been little discussion of the problem of providing them with the social and institutional 'infrastructure' as necessary preconditions for the take-off. On the contrary, much of the discussion proceeds on the implicit assumption that all the underdeveloped countries are ready for the take-off, as though a sufficiently long runway had already been built and that what is needed is a final spurt of speed on it. The dangers of a premature attempt to take off may be at least as great as those of a delayed take-off. It can result not only in wastages of scarce resources wrongly or inefficiently invested but also in a sense of disappointment and frustration which may have far-reaching psychological and political consequences.

So the second thing we should bear in mind about the underdeveloped countries is that they are not only of different types but are also at different stages of development. It is much more difficult to distinguish their different stages of development

B

because more subtle and qualitative factors are involved. Nevertheless, we should do our best to guard against trying to apply theories and policies appropriate for the more advanced types of underdeveloped countries to the more backward types, and vice versa.

Let us now turn to a somewhat different set of complications; these may be conveniently introduced by considering the question of the *widening gap* in per capita incomes between the developed and the underdeveloped countries. Considering the existing gap in incomes, and assuming a slower rate of growth for the underdeveloped countries, many writers have been alarmed by the possibility of this gap widening. What is more, they believe that this is even more dangerous and undesirable than the existing low absolute levels of income in the underdeveloped countries. Other writers deny the inevitability of the widening gap by pointing to the fact that some underdeveloped countries are growing just as fast or even faster than the developed countries. Now arithmetically, the widening gap depends not only on the difference in rates of growth but also on the initial width of the gap. We cannot say that the gap will not widen even for those underdeveloped countries whose per capita incomes are growing at a faster rate than those of the developed countries. This can be illustrated by a simple calculation of the gap between a developed country with a per capita income of $1,000 and an underdeveloped country with a per capita income of $100, both growing at the same rate, say 2% per annum. The initial gap is $900. Next year, the per capita income of the developed country rises to $1,020 while the per capita income of the underdeveloped country rises only to $102—thus resulting in a widening gap of $918. In fact the per capita income of the underdeveloped country must grow by 20% or ten times faster to get to $120 and maintain the same gap of $900.

Now comes the interesting question: provided that the per

capita incomes of the underdeveloped countries are rising, however slowly, or not falling absolutely, why is it more dangerous and alarming to have a widening relative gap? One would have thought that in terms of the evils of poverty such as hunger and disease, or even the 'vicious circle', it was the low absolute level of per capita income which mattered more than the size of the relative gap in incomes. Here at last we have reached those complications which are never far below the surface in the subject of the underdeveloped countries. It turns out that when people say that something should be done urgently to relieve the 'poverty' of the underdeveloped countries so as to ease international tensions, they are really concerned not with one problem, but with two distinct problems. On the one hand, there is what may be called the objective problem of poverty which may be measured by the absolute level of per capita income. On the other hand, there is the subjective problem of the discontent of the underdeveloped countries with their present economic status which far transcends this simple measurement. For this arises not only from their inability to fulfil economic desires, such as the desire to imitate the high standards both of private consumption and public social welfare, but also from the psychological and political drives to raise their national prestige and obtain equal status with the developed countries.

Perhaps even the widening relative gap in per capita incomes between the developed and the underdeveloped countries is merely a symbolic measurement of the underdeveloped countries' subjective level of discontent, for there is no close relationship between it and the objectively measurable level of poverty. Because of this, poorer rural communities in the underdeveloped countries where the traditional social structure is more intact seem to be less discontented than richer urban centres with a greater problem of adjustment to the new outside forces. Similarly, some of the seemingly most discontented underdeveloped countries are those which are relatively better off and are therefore able to appreciate and resent the gap between themselves and the advanced countries more keenly. Moreover, this feeling of discontent is reinforced by beliefs and theories about how their past pattern of economic development based on the expansion of primary exports has contributed to their present economic plight. In so far as this wholesale reaction against the past leads them to adopt policies of extreme economic nationalism which adversely affect their present economic situation, the sense of grievance is aggravated.

The third thing to bear in mind, therefore, is that the 'problem of poverty' of the underdeveloped countries is not a single problem, but a complex of problems, both subjective and objective. It is not sufficient to advocate general development policies, both to relieve their material poverty on humanitarian grounds and to ease subjective discontent and international tensions on political grounds, without further specifying which particular type of problem we are especially concerned with. International tensions can arise both from low material incomes and from the discontent created by 'the revolution of rising expectations', impatient for quick results. Economic development plans, however, are generally of a long-term nature, involving a considerable time-lag before their fruits are ready. In the meantime they may create a considerable amount of dislocation, discomfort and deprivation for the people without producing quick benefits. Contrary to popular belief, the vigorous pursuit of economic development policies designed to raise the level of material income in the future may frequently intensify, rather than reduce, the existing level of discontent in the developing countries.

I began by saying that there are two main forces behind the study of the underdeveloped countries—the desire to find the nature and causes of their poverty and the desire to show the need to do something urgently about it. Post-war writings on the subject have been dominated by the second motive. This is true not only of the voluminous and expanding literature produced by the various agencies of the United Nations and other governmental bodies, but also of the writings of the academic economists themselves. Faced with the pressing human and political problems of the underdeveloped countries, they also became impatient with impartial systematic inquiry and have taken on the role of champions and spokesmen for the underdeveloped countries. This is morally admirable and has also yielded valuable practical results. But its effect is not wholly fortunate from the point of view of the development of the subject as an academic discipline. The subject still gives the impression of having been written up originally to make a persuasive case for increasing international aid to the underdeveloped countries (although this tendency was strongest in the early 1950s and now there are signs of breaking away from it). So it is not unfair to say that there is still a considerable amount of loose, ambiguous and emotive argument, and shifting the basis of the argument from economic analysis to various types of value judgement ranging from humanitarian considerations to national self-interest. Moreover, it is no accident that the whole subject has come to be dominated by a monolithic theoretical model based on a particular type of country such as India which is not only suffering from acute population pressure and material poverty, but also possesses a sufficiently developed political and institutional framework to be able to carry out complicated large-scale economic development programmes with a reasonable chance of success; for this represents the strongest case for increasing international aid. There is nothing wrong with concentrating on this type of underdeveloped country, provided it is explicitly recognized as a particular case and not treated implicitly and uncritically as a prototype of all underdeveloped countries.

The aim of this book is to give an introduction to the economics of the underdeveloped or the developing countries using the traditional academic approach. Instead of trying to apply a single theoretical model to all underdeveloped countries, I shall use alternative models of analysis to give a more balanced picture of the different types of underdeveloped country at different stages of development. Instead of merely urging the underdeveloped countries to pursue economic development policies more vigorously and urging the advanced countries to give more aid for this purpose, I shall try to examine more carefully the logical basis of the arguments for these development policies, and consider how far they are appropriate for the circumstances of the different types of underdeveloped country. Facts and figures are given wherever necessary to provide the general background and the broad orders of magnitude. But on the whole, I shall be mainly concerned with the theoretical elements of the subject, particularly those relating to the problems of long-term economic development.

2

The Expansion of
Exports and the Growth of Population

The opening up of the underdeveloped countries

A popular idea of the underdeveloped country is of a closed society stagnating in traditional isolation, like Tibet before the Chinese annexation. Paradoxically enough, such a society in complete isolation would have few of the typical problems of the present-day underdeveloped countries. It would have a low and stagnant income per capita, but this would not matter if its inhabitants were blissfully unaware of the higher standards of living in the outside world. With no foreign trade, it would not have the problem of dependence on a few primary export commodities whose prices fluctuate violently in the world market. With no foreign enterprises operating within it, and no colonial rule, it would be free from real or imaginary grievances against 'foreign economic domination' and 'colonial exploitation'. And with a high death rate to match a high birth rate, it would not have to contend with the problem of population pressure as the population would be fairly stable or fluctuating around a constant size.

In contrast, the typical problems of the present-day underdeveloped countries arise, not because these countries are in the traditional state of isolation, but because they have been 'opened up' to outside forces, in the form of foreign trade, investment and colonial rule. The expansion of export production and the spread of the money economy have disrupted in varying degrees the economic self-sufficiency of the traditional 'subsistence economy'. The introduction of an orderly framework of administration by the colonial governments and the provision of basic public services, especially public health, have reduced the death rates, and caused a rapid growth of population. This has disrupted the traditional balance between population, natural resources and technology. Of course, the traditional society still persists in varying degrees in most underdeveloped countries in the form of the 'subsistence sector', and, as we shall see, this dominates the economic life of many countries, particularly in Africa. But it is still true to say that the typical present-day problems of these countries arise, not from traditional isolation but from modern changes. In a sense all underdeveloped countries are at different stages in the long transition period (or the 'pre-take-off' period) in which they are having to adapt to a continuing process of rapid and disruptive changes. Their problems arise from their difficulties in making satisfactory adjustments to these changes.

In this chapter I shall make a preliminary survey of the two major forces of change which have had and still continue to have a profound impact on the economic and social life of the underdeveloped countries. The first is the expansion of primary exports and the growth of the money economy. The second is the growth of population.

Expansion of exports

I shall begin by clearing up two points about the expansion of primary exports from the underdeveloped countries.

First, it is frequently described as the 'nineteenth century' pattern of international trade. Those who use this epithet may merely mean that it is associated with the nineteenth-century belief in free trade, but the general impression created is that the expansion of primary exports from the underdeveloped countries was historically important only in the nineteenth century. This is rather misleading. It is true that this process started in the latter half of the nineteenth century and owed much to the nineteenth-century revolution in transport such as the railways, the steamship, and, in the case of the Asian countries whose exports expanded fastest during this period, to the opening of the Suez Canal. But what is not generally realized is that the greatest expansion of primary exports from the underdeveloped countries of Africa and Latin America has taken place in the first half of the twentieth century. Contrary to the general impression that primary export expansion slackened off in the inter-war period, P. Lamartine Yates has calculated that the African and Latin American countries have expanded the total value of their exports ten-fold during the period 1913–53.[1]

Secondly, the primary exporting countries and the under-developed countries are frequently identified with each other, and the relative prices between primary exports as a whole and manufactured exports as a whole have been used to measure the gains from international trade to the underdeveloped countries. This again is not accurate. While all underdeveloped countries may be primary exporters, not all primary exporters are underdeveloped countries. The high-income countries of Australasia and North America are also important primary exporters. As a matter of fact, in 1913 the share of Asia, Africa and Latin America in the total value of the world's primary exports (excluding iron curtain countries) was only about 35%. It rose, however, to about 40% by 1928 and was about 46% in 1937. In the post-war year of 1953 it was about 47%.[2]

Although the underdeveloped countries as a group contribute less than half of the world's primary exports, there can

1. P. Lamartine Yates, *Forty Years of Foreign Trade*, Table 102, pp. 160–2.
2. Op. cit., Table 19, p. 47.

be no doubt that individually most of them are highly dependent on a few primary exports. Apart from exceptionally large countries such as China and India, exports form more than 10% of the national income of most underdeveloped countries. In 1953, there were at least thirteen underdeveloped countries which had ratios of merchandise trade to national income above 33%, and another six countries for which this ratio ranged between 20% and 33%. Moreover, the degree of dependence seems to have been increasing in the last few decades— in 1913 there were only nineteen underdeveloped countries who obtained more than 50% of their export receipts from one commodity; in 1953 there were no less than thirty countries in this situation.[1]

With this high degree of dependence on a few major exports, the underdeveloped countries are very vulnerable to the fluctuations in the world market prices of these exports. A recent United Nations report has estimated that, making allowance for the trend, the year-to-year fluctuations in the export receipts of the underdeveloped countries during 1948–58 have averaged between 9% and 12%, some countries having an average fluctuation of 18%.[2]

The problem of the underdeveloped 'export economies' which has received widespread attention is the problem of economic instability, and vulnerability to the violent fluctuations in the world market prices of primary products. In the short run, this is clearly the most serious problem facing many underdeveloped countries. It not only introduces a serious instability into the consumption and living standards of these countries but also creates formidable difficulties for maintain-

1. P. Lamartine Yates, op. cit, Table A 104, p. 163, excluding South Africa and Japan. But one should add Northern and Southern Rhodesia and Kenya to the list of countries with ratios of exports to national income higher than 33%. See also Tables 120, 121 and 122, pp. 179–81.

2. *International Compensations for Fluctuations in Commodity Trade*, New York 1961, pp. 3–5.

ing a steady flow of investment for long-term economic development. But we cannot obtain a complete picture of the impact of the outside economic forces on the underdeveloped countries without going beyond this familiar short-term problem of overall economic instability to two further deep-seated problems.

The first problem is the relation between the expansion of primary exports and the long-term economic development of the underdeveloped countries. Some of the orthodox economists were inclined to assume too readily that the expansion of international trade would automatically transmit economic growth to the underdeveloped countries, and the 'specialization' in the production of those primary products most suited to their resources would automatically raise their general level of skills and productivity and lead to a more productive combination of resources. This would pave the way for further economic development. Nowadays, the pendulum has swung to the opposite extreme, not only among the political leaders of the developing countries but among professional economists also. It is now generally assumed that the expansion of primary exports is highly unlikely ever to provide a satisfactory basis of continuous economic growth for the underdeveloped countries. I shall examine not only the older generalization but also the newer generalization which is a reaction against the older view.

The second problem arises from the fact that the expansion of primary exports in the underdeveloped countries generally took place through the agency of foreign-owned enterprises operating within these countries and, until recently, under colonial rule for most of the Asian and African countries. The problem of the relationship between the expansion of primary exports and long-term economic development is therefore considerably complicated by the problems of subjective discontent concerning 'foreign economic domination' and 'colonial exploitation'. To study these problems I shall have to go beyond the overall values of the exports of the underdeveloped countries as geographical units, and analyse how the proceeds from these geographical exports were distributed between foreign and domestic participants in export production. In the case of peasant export commodities, the participants were the foreign export-import firms and the domestic peasant producers. In the case of mining and plantation exports, the foreign participation covered not only capital investment and skilled labour but also in many cases unskilled labour from other underdeveloped countries; the domestic participation was mainly confined to such indigenous unskilled labour as might be employed in the mines and plantations. These different patterns and the differing extent of domestic participation in export production are important, not only from the point of view of income distribution but also from the point of view of long-term economic development. First, the distribution of incomes between the foreign and domestic participants would have some effect on the proportion of incomes reinvested locally and spent on domestically produced goods, compared with the 'leakages' abroad in the form of imports and remittances of the earnings of the foreign participants. Secondly, if we wish to find out how far the expansion of primary export production has affected the skills and productivity of the indigenous people of the underdeveloped countries, we shall have to go beyond the pattern of distribution of incomes to the distribution of productive activities and economic roles. We can then look for the particular features in the past pattern of primary export expansion that have been unfavourable for the maintenance of long-term economic growth, and consider whether these characteristic features are the inevitable concomitant of future expansion in primary export production for some of the underdeveloped countries.

With these questions in view, I shall devote the next three

chapters to the study of the expansion of exports first from the peasant sector and then from the mining and plantation sector. I shall outline the typical patterns of the growth of the market economy, not only in the markets for commodities but also in the markets for labour and capital funds. I shall start from the early phase of export expansion and bring the story up to the present time when the reaction against the past economic pattern has led to various nationalistic policies of economic development being adopted by the governments of the newly independent developing countries.

The growth of population

Let us now turn to the other major change which has affected the underdeveloped countries—the growth of population. An underdeveloped country in its traditional state of isolation tends to have a fairly stable population with a high birth rate and a high death rate balancing out over the long run. Although accurate information is not available, the most probable estimate seems to be that, before their contact with the West, many underdeveloped countries in Asia and Africa had high birth rates in the region of 4% per annum matched by equally high death rates of about 4%. Starting from the initial position of high birth and death rates, I shall describe the typical pattern of population growth with three stages or sets of factors that reduce the death rate while the birth rate continues at its high initial level.[1]

First, the introduction of a modern administration improving law and order and eliminating local warfare, and the introduction of modern transport and communication eliminating local famines and spreading trading in foodstuffs, can by themselves reduce the death rate of an underdeveloped country by as much as 1% per annum. So if the birth rate remains unchanged,

1. Cf. W. A. Lewis, *The Theory of Economic Growth*, Ch. 6.

population will be increasing at 1% per annum. Secondly, the introduction of public health measures controlling epidemic and endemic diseases such as plague, smallpox, cholera, malaria, yellow fever (and eventually tuberculosis) can reduce the death rate by at least another 1%. So if the birth rate remains the same, the population of the underdeveloped country will be increasing at some 2% per annum at the end of this second stage. Thirdly, the spread of individual medical attention and the increase in the number of doctors and hospitals can bring down the death rate by another 1%, depending on the age structure of the population. In this final stage, therefore, if the birth rate remains the same at 4% and the death rate is reduced to 1% per annum, the maximum possible rate of growth in population will approach 3% per annum.

Most of the underdeveloped countries have passed through the first stage and are either towards the end of the second stage with the rate of population increase between $1\frac{1}{2}$% and 2% per annum or are well into the third stage with the rate of population increase over 2%. The fastest rate of population growth is to be found in Latin America with an average annual rate of growth of 2·4%, while Asia and Africa are fast approaching the 2% rate of growth. India, which until the last census in 1961 had a population growth of 1·4%, now seems to have passed the 2% mark, mainly due to better control of malaria. There are still a few Asian countries at the lower end of the $1\frac{1}{2}$%–2% range such as Burma, with her high rate of infant mortality, and possibly China which many authorities believe to have a relatively slow rate of population growth. But for most of the underdeveloped countries, a 2% rate of population growth is typical, giving us a possibility of the population doubling every thirty-five years.[1] So when people speak of the 'population explosion' in the underdeveloped countries, they mean that the populations of these countries are not only

1. United Nations *Demographic Yearbooks*.

increasing but increasing at a faster rate of growth year by year with a high rate of acceleration. An extreme example of this is the case of Ceylon where D.D.T. has wiped out malaria, reducing the death rate from 2·2% to 1·2% in seven years from 1945 to 1952—a fall which took seventy years in England and Wales.[1]

✓ Although the rate of population growth is clearly very important, two other factors must be taken into account in studying the problem of population pressure in the under-developed countries.

The first is the population density in relation to natural resources and technology. Population density in a significant sense cannot be measured simply by taking the number of people per square mile. It will depend on a number of factors such as the quality of agricultural land, climate and water supply, the existence of mineral resources, the possibilities of hydro-electric power, to name a few; and also, very import-antly, on the level of productivity and technology. Europe and Asia, for example (excluding U.S.S.R. from both), are esti-mated to have the same amount of agricultural area per person of 1·5 acres, but with widely differing standards of living or 'population densities' in the economic sense. But taking the level of technology to mean the indigenous methods of agri-cultural production and making allowances for obvious differences in natural resources, it is still possible to say that there are very significant differences in population densities between the different parts of the underdeveloped world. Com-pared, for example, with the agricultural area per person of 1·5 acres in Asia, Latin America is estimated to have 6·9 acres, and Africa 10·6 acres of agricultural area per person.[2] In a relatively sparsely populated region like Latin America, even a high population growth rate will not for the time being give

1. P.E.P., *World Population and Resources*, p. 12.
2. P.E.P., op. cit., p. 50, and Chs. 2 and 3.

rise to the problem of population pressure. In fact, many would regard it as a favourable factor for future economic development. In contrast, with the dense population of China even a small population growth rate will create formidable problems of population pressure.

There are two main types of underdeveloped country with high population densities. Firstly, there are the long settled agricultural countries such as India, China or Egypt. In a sense, their present population problem is due to their successful development as agricultural countries in the past. This enabled them to support a dense population before it started growing in the modern period. Secondly, there are the island plantation economies, such as the West Indies, Fiji, Mauritius or Ceylon. Here, immigrant labour has been brought from outside to work in the mines and plantations to add to the indigenous population. Population pressure subsequently developed, helped by the relative ease with which diseases such as malaria can be wiped out from the islands. In general, the first group of countries tend to have a larger population base than the second —contrast India's 438 millions in 1961 with Mauritius' 0·6 million.

This brings us to the second important factor to be taken into account in studying the population problems of the underdeveloped countries, that is the absolute size of the population base. When giving aid, countries like India with a huge population base clearly present a more formidable problem than countries with a smaller population, even if the smaller populations are increasing at a faster rate. Even before 1951, when the rate of increase was relatively slow, India's population was increasing at the rate of 5 millions a year: with the new, higher rate of 2·15% per annum shown by the 1961 Census, it will be increasing at the rate of 8 millions a year. The size of the population base, however, is also of great importance as it affects the total scale of the economy; this is relevant for the success of industrialization programmes. Of course, the size of the domestic market of a country does not depend only on the numbers, but also on the income level of its inhabitants. But given the same low level of per capita incomes, a country like India offers a more favourable environment for setting up heavy capital goods industries which depend so much on the economies of scale for their success. In contrast, a thickly populated country with a small population base such as Ceylon seems to be especially handicapped by the smallness of its market.[1] Finally, considering the absolute size of the population base serves to remind us that while the large populations of the advanced countries have grown up after, and as a consequence of, economic development, the large populations of the underdeveloped countries exist before development: this makes development not only more desirable but also more difficult.[2]

In broad terms, the population problem of the densely populated underdeveloped countries is a vivid illustration of the Malthusian theory. On a closer analysis, I would add three qualifications.

(i) The Malthusian proposition that the growth of population will exceed the growth of food supplies underrates technological innovations in food production, including the opening up of new territories and international trade. That was why the advanced Western countries were able to escape from its direful predictions. In a sense, the theories of economic development for the overpopulated underdeveloped countries are built on this qualification. They are based on the idea that while there is a maximum limit to population growth, say 3% per annum, the possible rate of increase in output owing to

1. J. R. Hicks, *Essays in World Economics*, pp. 207–8.
2. S. Kuznets, *Underdeveloped Countries and the Pre-industrial Phase in the Advanced Countries*, World Population Conference, 1954 Papers, vol. V.

C

technical innovation and capital accumulation can exceed this maximum rate of population growth, keeping the Malthusian Devil at bay until the birth rates in the underdeveloped countries begin to fall, as they have fallen in the European countries and are falling in countries like Japan.

(ii) The Malthusian theory is based on too rigid a causal connection between the rate of growth in food supply and population growth. According to the theory, population will not grow unless the food supply or the standard of living rises above the minimum subsistence level. But as we have seen, the population in many underdeveloped countries has grown very rapidly without any appreciable rise in per capita income, mainly owing to medical improvements reducing death rates. If the Malthusian theory has underrated the possibilities of technical improvements in food production, it has also underrated the medical improvements reducing death rates. The possibility that even a population struggling at a minimum subsistence level could grow in the short run simply by medical improvements entirely unconnected with the general standard of life adds to the seriousness of the problem in the modern setting. There is a gleam of hope, however, if we are willing to believe that the technical improvements in medicine which are at present reducing death rates only can be eventually extended to reduce birth rates by the invention of simpler and cheaper methods of birth-control.

(iii) The Malthusian theory is formulated in the setting of a more or less developed wage economy. According to it, with given natural resources and technology, the saturation point in a country's population will be reached when the level of wages, determined by the marginal product of labour, is equal to the minimum subsistence level. But in many underdeveloped countries, the problem of population pressure takes place in the setting of the subsistence economy before the development of the money and the wage economy. In this setting, with an extended family system, many people whose marginal product on the land is below the subsistence level can continue to exist at that level because the total output from land is shared among the members of the extended family. That is to say, with the same natural resources and technology, the saturation point of population in a subsistence economy is larger than that of a wage economy (without public poor relief) because it is determined by the equality of the average product of labour to the minimum subsistence level. Many people who would have been unemployed and starved in a wage economy are maintained in 'disguised' unemployment by their relatives as part of a traditional social security system. As we shall see, much has been made of this phenomenon of 'disguised unemployment' in the post-war theories of economic development as a concealed source of saving. But there is one point which is not always appreciated. In so far as we believe that economic development can take place only through the introduction of a modern money and wage economy which entails the dismantling of the traditional social security system of the subsistence economy, the overpopulated underdeveloped countries in a process of transition have to meet a double problem of population increase. In addition to their natural rate of increase in population they also have to find jobs for those who are displaced from the subsistence economy when the development of the exchange economy and economic individualism reduces the size of the 'family' as a social security unit.

To sum up, the problem of population pressure in the underdeveloped countries has three aspects: (i) the rate of growth of the population; (ii) the existing density of population; and (iii) the overall magnitude of the population base. In these terms, the population situation in the underdeveloped countries shows considerable variation. At one end of the scale there are the underdeveloped countries which are relatively thinly populated and are not yet suffering from population pressure. These include some of the South-East Asian countries such as Burma, Thailand, Malaysia and the Outer Islands of Indonesia; many of the African countries with the notable exception of Egypt; and most of the Latin American countries. The magnitude of the population base in these countries is also small and is below 50 millions, with the exception of Brazil, which is, however, still thinly populated. At the other end of the scale there are the densely populated countries suffering from varying degrees of population pressure. These include islands with plantation economies such as the West Indies, Mauritius and Ceylon where the population pressure is acute although the magnitude of the population base is fairly small; and the thickly populated countries of Asia and the Middle East with much larger population bases. The population pressure problem is most formidable in countries like India and Pakistan which are not only densely populated, but have a large population base and are now entering into a phase of rapid population growth above the 2% annual rate.

Post-war theories about the developing countries tend to be dominated by the model of the overpopulated countries. But large areas of the underdeveloped world such as Latin America, South-East Asia and various parts of Africa started with sparse populations in relation to their natural resources and are not yet suffering from population pressure. We need, therefore, at least two main theoretical models, one for the countries with no significant population pressure, and another for the over-populated countries. For certain purposes involving the analysis of the economies of scale, we shall find it useful to subdivide the overpopulated countries into two groups: those like India with a large population base, say over 50 millions; and those like Ceylon and Mauritius with a small population base.

In the next two chapters, I shall be mainly working on the basis of the model of the underdeveloped countries without significant population pressure. I have done this not only to give a more balanced picture of the subject, which is normally dominated by the model of the overpopulated countries, but also because the important structural problems arising out of the growth of the money economy and the wage economy through the expansion of primary export production can be most clearly seen when isolated from the problem of population pressure. I shall return to the model of overpopulated countries when we examine the post-war theories of economic development in Chapters 6, 7, and 8.

3

Peasant Exports and the Growth
of the Money Economy

The importance of the peasant sector

Although peasant exports such as rice, cocoa, palm oil or cotton have a modest share in the total value of primary exports from the underdeveloped world as a whole,[1] it is important to study the expansion of peasant export production for at least three reasons.

First, peasant families, combining the roles of consumers and producers, are the basic units of the subsistence economy and are therefore of central importance in studying the impact of outside economic forces on the people of the underdeveloped countries. In addition, the expansion of peasant exports is one of the best documented parts of the process of economic change in the underdeveloped countries, and we can build up a fairly clear picture of the response of the indigenous people to economic incentives. This gives us a good basis to judge

1. Important peasant exports are confined to a few countries of Asia and Africa, such as Burma, Thailand, Ghana, Nigeria, Uganda, etc. Latin America has little or no peasant exports. The importance of the mines and plantations in the total primary exports of the underdeveloped countries as a group can be seen from the fact that in 1953, the mineral products alone contributed to over a third of the total primary exports of the group. Among agricultural products, plantation output dominates in the exports of coffee, sugar, tea, sisal, etc. Rubber is a predominantly plantation export although smallholders in Malaya contribute an important part of the output. Cocoa and palm oil, which are peasant products in West Africa, are plantation products in Brazil, Indonesia and Malaya. Cf. P. Lamartine Yates, op. cit., Table A 32, p. 240.

various generalizations about the economic behaviour of the
people of the underdeveloped countries in other contexts.

Secondly, from the viewpoint of the indigenous people in
the subsistence economy, peasant production is the main alternative to wage employment, not only in the mines and plantations, but also in manufacturing industry. Thus the major process of economic development by which labour from the subsistence economy is drawn into wage employment cannot be
studied without taking into account the alternative opportunities (or lack of them) as self-employed peasant producers.

Thirdly, the expansion of peasant export production is so
important and spectacular in a number of Asian and African
underdeveloped countries that it is worth studying for its own
sake. For instance, using 1870 as the base, the value of peasant
rice exports from Burma and Thailand increased some 10 to
13 times by 1913, and up to about 20 times in the late 1920s
before the onset of the Great Depression. Similarly, the value
of Ghana's cocoa exports increased about 13 times during the
1913–53 period. During the same period Nigeria expanded her
exports of oil and oil seeds by 7 times in addition to a very
rapid expansion of cocoa exports. In all these countries, the
physical output of the export crops followed a characteristic
growth curve, rising steeply in the early phase and tapering off
gradually.[1]

This rapid expansion of the peasant export sector is all the

1. Cf. J. S. Furnivall, *Colonial Policy and Practice*, Appendix I; J. C.
Ingram, *Economic Change in Thailand since 1850*, Ch. 3 and Appendix C;
P. Lamartine Yates, op. cit., pp. 242–3; and the West African Institute of
Economic Research, *Annual Conference*, Economic Section, Achimota
1953, pp. 96–7. Peasant exports contributed two-thirds of Burma's
total exports up to 1937 and dominate her post-war exports with the decline of output from the foreign-owned mines and plantations. Cocoa contributed 50% to the value of Ghana's total exports in 1913 and 70% in
1953. Oil and oil seeds contributed 78% to the total value of Nigeria's
exports in 1913. In 1953 oil and oil seeds and cocoa contributed 70% to her
total exports.

more interesting because, unlike that of the mining and planta-tion sector, it seems to owe little or nothing to outside economic resources. (i) Most of the foreign investment in the under-developed countries flowed into the mining and plantation sector where the major part of the capital requirement took the form of expensive durable equipment and fixed capital. In con-trast, apart from land, peasant production required very little durable capital equipment. Its major capital requirement took the form of circulating capital or the 'subsistence fund' of food and consumers' goods required to maintain the peasants until the harvest was ready. As we shall see, in its early phase of expansion, peasant export production appears to have been largely 'self-financing'. Further problems of capital and finan-cing of the peasant sector will be taken up in Chapter 5. (ii) While the mining and plantation sector represents the extension of modern economic organization and technology, the peasant export sector seems to be simply an extension of the traditional economic organization and technology of the subsistence economy. Rice exports from South-East Asia, for example, represent the traditional subsistence crop whose cultivation has been expanded by traditional methods for the export market. Even in West Africa where cocoa was a new crop (introduced by peasant enterprise) the secret of its success was that it did not require a radical departure from the methods of subsistence agriculture and could therefore be readily grafted on to the traditional economy.[1] (iii) While the mining and plantation sector usually recruited a large part of their unskilled labour from outside the countries in which they were located, peasant export expansion required little or no labour from abroad. In fact, the bulk of the labour was supplied from the family circle of the peasant producers. The size of the peasant holdings was usually not large enough to require hired labour from outside except in very busy seasons such as the harvest. Further, the

1. A. Macphee, *The Economic Revolution in West Africa*, pp. 39–40.

'family' in peasant societies embraced an extensive network of more distant relatives. For these reasons hired wage labour from outside the family circle did not become important in the peasant export sector until a later stage,[1] although there was some development of wage labour in the ancillary industries which went with peasant export expansion, such as transport and processing—for instance rice milling in South-East Asia.

The mechanics of peasant export expansion

How then did this very rapid process of expansion take place? Two things were necessary to start the process. The first was the improvement in transport and communications opening up the remoter districts (and incidentally improving the law and order in these parts); the second was the establishment of foreign export-import firms to act as the middlemen between the peasants and the world market. The improvement in transport and communications was overwhelmingly important in many countries. The export-import firms performed two functions: to collect, process and transport the peasant produce to the foreign buyers, and to offer the peasants the inducement to increase export production by selling them imported goods. This inducement to the peasants was as important, perhaps even more important, than the other function of the firms. For in this early phase of international trade, imports were not merely a cheaper way of satisfying the *existing* wants of the peasants. Many of them were novelties hitherto unknown in the subsistence economy. By stimulating new wants among the peasants, the expansion of imports was a major dynamic force facilitating the expansion of exports. The speed with which the

1. In Ghana, the most highly developed peasant export economy in Africa, the ratio of family labour to hired labour in cocoa production was estimated to be about 5:1 in 1950 (U.N. Report on the *Enlargement of the Exchange Economy in Tropical Africa*, p. 31). Hired labour, paid in kind at harvest, was used in Burmese rice production.

peasants of South-East Asia and West Africa (with their different cultural backgrounds) acquired the taste for the new imported commodities and expanded their export production in order to be able to buy them offers us concrete evidence of their capacity to respond positively to economic incentives. It casts serious doubt on popular generalizations about the limited wants and the inability of the people to respond to economic incentives. We shall meet these generalizations when we consider the factors determining the wage level in the mining and plantation sector.

With these two initial factors—the improvement in transport and communications, and the existence of the foreign export-import firms to get the peasants in touch with the world market —peasant export production expanded rapidly by extending cultivation in widening circles into the hinterland of the country. On the supply side, there were two other factors which enabled peasant export expansion to grow so quickly and on so large a scale. The first was of course the existence of unused hinterland, the jungles which could be cleared to grow the export crop. It was no accident that all the Asian and African countries which were to develop into important peasant export economies started before the expansion of trade with relatively sparse population and abundant supply of 'semi-empty' hinterland. The second concerned the source of the labour supply, which requires more careful analysis.

I have said that peasant export production did not rely on large-scale immigrant labour from abroad, and that it did not introduce any drastic changes in methods of agriculture, such as labour-saving techniques. Yet the physical output of peasant exports grew most rapidly, well above any possible natural rate of increase in working population, in the early phase of expansion when most of the labour requirement must have been supplied from within the peasant families. This suggests that initially there must have been a considerable amount of underemployed or surplus labour in these families. At first sight, this may appear surprising since the idea of rural underemployment or 'disguised unemployment' is nowadays only associated with overpopulated countries where there is insufficient work for every member of the family on the overcrowded land. But the cause of the rural underemployment which must have existed in the thinly populated peasant societies before they were opened up to trade was quite different. There was abundant waste land waiting to be cultivated, but labour remained underemployed because there was a lack of effective demand for its potential increase in output. In the initial situation, with the available surplus land and surplus labour, and with the traditional methods of cultivation, a peasant family could have produced a much larger agricultural output than it was actually producing for its own subsistence consumption. But it chose not to do so, for the simple reason that every other peasant family could do the same and there would be no one in the locality who would want to buy the surplus output. With the poor transport and communications and the rudimentary exchange system which existed before the opening up of the export trade, the local and domestic market of the underdeveloped countries was too narrow and unorganized to absorb their potential surplus agricultural output. At this stage, therefore, the main function of international trade was to create effective demand: it linked up the world market demand for the type of things which the peasants could produce with the surplus productive capacity the peasants had locked up in the subsistence economy.

Two concepts of the subsistence sector and the two stages of the money economy

At this stage it is necessary to distinguish the two possible meanings of the term 'subsistence' economy or sector. It can mean that the economic units within it such as the family, the village or the tribe, are self-sufficient, producing only what they require for their own consumption, and having little or no systematic exchange relationship among each other. This is the sense in which we have been using the term so far, and in our context 'subsistence' simply means non-monetary. The term also carries the suggestion that the people within the subsistence sector are living at a 'minimum subsistence level': that is to say, the resources and the technology they possess are just sufficient to keep them alive in their present numbers at the minimum level of subsistence. Clearly, the 'subsistence' sector in the first sense does not necessarily mean that the people within it are struggling at the 'minimum subsistence level' in the second sense. Indeed, the rapid expansion in exports we have been describing could not really have taken place had these particular peasant societies been really at the minimum subsistence level in the true sense before trade was opened to them. The essential lubricant which pushed the peasants so smoothly and rapidly into export production and the money economy was the existence of a considerable margin of surplus productive capacity in the form of both surplus land and surplus labour over and above their minimum subsistence requirements.

With this margin of surplus productive capacity, the peasants could take to the production of cash crops for the export market *without* reducing their subsistence output. In the South-East Asian countries, where rice was both a subsistence and an export crop, the question of reducing subsistence production did not arise. The subsistence crops of African peasant economies could either be interplanted with their export crops (such as cocoa trees) before they reached a certain age, or cultivated in rotation with export crops such as cotton and groundnuts. With the exception of Ghana in recent years, the normal pattern in many African countries still seems to be for the output of the subsistence crops and the cash crops for export to expand together.[1] In the early phase of export expansion, therefore, what the peasants were in effect doing was taking up export production as a part-time activity to obtain an extra cash income, in addition to their subsistence production of which they had already made sure. This cash income could then be spent on extra luxury items of consumption in the form of imported goods. The expansion of export production at this phase was a virtually riskless operation, requiring no other cost than extra working hours which could be provided from the initial situation of underemployment. Because, as we have seen, the 'capital requirement' in peasant production consisted mainly in the 'subsistence fund' to tide over the producers until the harvest, export expansion of this type could be mainly self-financing.

As a contrast, let us consider a different initial situation in which the peasants had to devote the whole of their time and resources to obtain a minimum subsistence level of living before the opening up of trade. Here, even if switching their resources from the subsistence to the cash crops promised some monetary gain, they would have been obliged to reduce their subsistence output to grow the export crop. This would have made their entry into export production and the money economy a hazardous undertaking with no margin to meet a possible risk of starvation if something went wrong with their cash crops. In this case, we should expect the peasants to be justifiably hesitant about leaving the security of their subsistence economy, and their export production, if any, would expand much more slowly than the actual rates of expansion we have observed in the peasant economies of South-East Asia and West Africa. This may partly account for the persistence of large subsistence

1. Cf. U.N. Report on the *Enlargement of the Exchange Economy*, cited above, pp. 21–2. 'Thus, in Uganda for example, where the estimates of the area under major crops are available for a number of years, the area under cotton increased between 1918 and 1950 about eleven-fold and the area under subsistence food crops about seven times.'

ctors in the overpopulated countries like India and Pakistan
.1 spite of the fact that they have been opened up to outside
economic forces much longer than the African countries. To
try to explain this entirely in terms of the 'conservatism' of
their peasants and social rigidities is not convincing since these
factors also operate in other peasant societies where export
production and the money economy have expanded at a much
faster rate. The size of the margin of surplus productive capacity over the minimum subsistence requirement in the subsistence sector therefore emerges as a very important factor
determining how quickly the subsistence sector can be drawn
into the money economy. I have emphasized the initial population density on land as one of the determinants of this surplus
productive capacity; but it also depends on other factors such
as the technical efficiency of the subsistence agriculture, or the
fertility and accessibility of the land under subsistence cultivation.

On this basis, I can now depict the spread of the money
economy and the expansion of peasant export production in
two analytically distinct phases, although they overlap a great
deal in practice. In the first phase, the money economy may be
considered as growing simply by bringing in an increasing
number of peasant families into export production, each family
producing the export crop on a spare-time basis while continuing to produce all its subsistence requirements. In the second
phase, however, some peasant families will begin to 'specialize' or devote the whole of their available resources to export
production, so setting up a cash demand for locally produced
foodstuffs and other locally produced goods and services.

These two phases in the growth of the money economy have
very different characteristics. The first phase offers certain
advantages to the peasants, since the export production is a
spare-time activity in addition to their subsistence production.
Imports represent a net increase in consumption and a rise in

the standard of living. And since their 'capital requirements' are largely provided out of the subsistence output, they are largely self-financing and need not resort to borrowing at high rates of interest from money-lenders. Similarly, their bargaining position with the middlemen is also stronger, since if the prices offered for their cash crops are not favourable, they can afford to reduce output next year (just enough to pay taxes, if any). There are two disadvantages, however, in partial commitment to the money economy. First, the peasants have not fully utilized the market opportunities open to them and could increase their income by greater 'specialization'. Secondly, the main function of money in this first phase is merely to exchange exports for imports. That is to say, the money economy is confined to foreign trade and has little or no impact on the rest of the domestic economy.

In contrast, in the second phase, the fact that some peasant families are devoting the whole of their available resources to export production obliges them to buy their food requirements from other peasant families who can now specialize in food production as a cash crop for the domestic market. That is to say, complete specialization in export production by some peasant families not only enables them to make full use of their available market opportunities, but also provides the scope for secondary rounds of economic activities which may spread widely into the rest of the economy. The money economy has now spread from the foreign trade sector to the domestic sector. Here, it may spread into the market for other locally produced consumers' goods industries in so far as they can compete with the imports. It may spread into the market for labour for these local industries and for peasant agriculture itself in so far as hired labour is required to supplement that of the family. It may spread into the market for land in so far as existing laws and customs permit free buying, selling and renting of land. These are the advantages, but the second phase in the growth of the money economy also brings to a head many of the problems latent in a situation in which peasants inexperienced in modern economic life are brought into rapid contact with the complexities of an unstable export market. In switching over from part-time to full-time production for the export market, the peasants cease to be self-financing and have to borrow from the chief source available to them—the moneylenders who charge them high rates of interest. With their ignorance of the rapidly changing market conditions, they tend to get heavily into debt, and where land is alienable, they lose their land in default of loans and get reduced to the status of tenants. And with their fixed and frequently heavy monetary obligations in the form of debts, rents, and also government taxes, they can no longer afford to reduce their output when the price is lowered; they may even try to produce more to make up for the lower price. But the inelastic nature of their supply curve aggravates the fall in the price of their export products. With this full (if sometimes involuntary) commitment to the money economy, the peasants now have a weaker bargaining position with the middlemen. In most peasant export economies, the middlemen, after a long chain of intermediaries, culminate in a few large export-import firms, each buying a large proportion of the total output of the peasants. At this stage, therefore, there is a real danger that a few foreign-owned firms would combine to exercise monopoly power over the peasants and shift on to them the main impact of the fall in the world market price for the export product.

Most of the African peasant economies, with the notable exception of Ghana, are still largely in the first phase of the growth of the money economy. The peasants there are only partially committed to the production of cash crops, and the larger proportion of their resources (about 70% of the total cultivated land and about 60% of the total adult male labour force for the whole of tropical Africa) is still used for subsistence production. Even in Nigeria and Uganda, which are the most developed African peasant economies after Ghana, over half their land and labour resources are still in the subsistence sector.[1] Similar conditions probably exist in the Indian peasant societies of Latin America whose exports are predominantly from the mining and plantation sector. The main reason for the existence of these large subsistence sectors seems to be lack of transport and communications, and the very poor marketing facilities available to the peasant. This type of subsistence sector in Africa which belongs to the early phase in the spread of the money economy may be contrasted with the subsistence sectors which have persisted in the overpopulated countries of Asia like India and Pakistan. These countries clearly do not belong to the early phase in the growth of the money economy in our sense. In fact, outside the subsistence sectors they have a fairly complex economic and monetary structure. They also have more developed systems of transport and communications than many African countries. So, as I have suggested, the main reason for their large subsistence sectors may be found in the overcrowding on land which has reduced the peasants to a minimum subsistence level, with no saleable surplus output to facilitate their entry into the money economy. In broad terms, therefore, we may distinguish two types of subsistence sector. The first type, characterizing most of the African peasant economies, is mainly caused by a lack of effective demand. The second type, characterized by the overpopulated peasant economies of Asia, is mainly caused by a lack of supply.

The second phase in the growth of the money economy in our sense is represented by the more developed peasant export economies, such as Burma, Thailand and Ghana. These countries still have a sizeable subsistence sector (about a quarter of

1. United Nations Report on the *Enlargement of the Exchange Economy*, cited above, Tables 4 and 6, pp. 14–17 and passim.

D

the total land and male labour employed in the case of Ghana), but a larger proportion of their peasants have been engaged in whole-time production for the export market for many decades and they have become fully committed to the money economy. This dependence on the export market can be seen from the fact that during the Great Depression of 1931 and the decade which followed it, it was the peasants in these countries who seem to have suffered most from the fluctuations in the export market, and complained most about the monopoly power of the foreign export-import firms. It is also significant that in the post-war period, and after their independence, both Burma and Ghana took enthusiastically to the system of marketing boards for the peasant exports. Burma has frankly used this system to nation-alize the foreign export-import firms which dominated her pre-war rice trade, and to obtain the revenue for financing her industrial development plans. Ghana's marketing board started with the official aim of stabilizing the peasants' incomes, but is tending towards the Burmese pattern, and becoming the chief source of revenue for economic development.

Peasant exports and economic development

There has been a considerable amount of controversy about how far the West African marketing boards have effectively stabilized peasant incomes, and how far the Burmese marketing board has exploited the peasants under the guise of protecting them from the middlemen. But beyond the problems of short-term economic stability and distribution of incomes, there is the long-term problem of how far the increase in peasant export production still offers a satisfactory basis for further economic development in these countries. A fuller answer to this question must wait until we consider the factors likely to affect the future trends in the world market demand for primary products in Chapter 9. But even at this stage it is possible to bring out a number of points which have emerged from our analysis of the supply side of the question.

I have shown that peasant export production expanded without the introduction of radical improvements in the agricultural techniques used in subsistence production, and that when the peasants took to 'specializing' in export crops it merely meant that they were devoting the whole of their resources to export production. In doing this they took full advantage of the *market opportunities* available to them; but this does not mean that they took full advantage of the *technical opportunities* to improve their productivity. Peasant holdings in rice production, for example, have remained approximately the same, and the same combination of land, labour and capital have been used throughout half a century of rapid expansion in rice exports from South-East Asia. The same thing is true of the West African cocoa exports. Although there are some large cocoa farmers with annual incomes above £500, on the whole the productivity of resources in the cocoa industry has remained constant.[1] This means that 'specialization' in these peasant export economies is not the same thing as 'specialization' as understood by Western economists who use the term to mean a greater degree of division of labour leading to higher productivity and economies of production. If this is true, then peasant export production continuing on the same basis as before is bound to come to a stop sooner or later, even if demand conditions continue to be favourable. Sooner or later the extension of cultivation will press against the limits of cultivable hinterland, and thereafter population growth will outstrip export expansion and lead to a situation of overpopulation and 'disguised unemployment' in agriculture.

1. W. A. Lewis, *Report on the Industrialization of the Gold Coast*, 1953, p. 3. For other cases of decline in productivity in peasant agriculture due to use of less suitable land, over-cropping and soil erosion, see Ingram, op. cit., pp. 49–50 and the U.N. Report on the *Enlargement of the Exchange Economy*, p. 22.

Two very different policy conclusions can be drawn from this. The first is that peasant export expansion is not likely to offer a satisfactory basis for a continuous and self-sustained type of economic development, and that therefore these countries should turn to manufacturing industry. This is the conclusion favoured by many of the newly independent developing countries in South-East Asia and Africa, although they do not so far suffer from overpopulation. Thus, they tend to divert the larger part of the proceeds from peasant exports obtained through the marketing boards and other forms of taxation to industrial development, so starving the peasant export sector of capital and technical assistance.[1] But an entirely different policy conclusion can also be drawn. The fact that peasant export production has not shown any technical improvements in the past does not mean that it is inherently incapable of improvement if adequate resources are ploughed back into it. The past pattern merely shows that these opportunities for improvements have been neglected because, with unused land easily available, it was so much easier to expand along existing lines than to try to introduce improved methods of production. Further, in so far as the peasant export economies of South-East Asia and Africa have not yet reached a state of over-population in relation to land, it will be necessary for them to raise productivity in peasant production if only to release the labour required for their industrialization. These two conflicting policy conclusions will be considered in Chapter 9.

1. An extreme case of this tendency was found until recently in the policy of the Burmese Government, which, like the Ghanaian Government, obtained on the average some 40% of its total revenue from the profits of the marketing board and other taxation on exports. Yet the only direct benefit which the Burmese peasants obtained from the earlier development plans were the subsidized agricultural loans which covered only about 16% of their total short-term credit requirements. Cf. Aye Hlaing, *Some Aspects of Seasonal Agricultural Loans in Burma*, pp. 3–5. See also Ghana's *Second Development Plan*, p. 62.

4

Mines and Plantations and the Growth of the Wage Economy

Mines and plantations are large-scale enterprises which normally require more labour per unit of land than peasant agriculture. They generally created a very large expansion in the demand for indigenous labour when they started their operations in the underdeveloped countries. This expansion in demand for labour could be met without difficulty in the countries which were already densely populated. But frequently the location of natural resources required the mines and plantations to be set up in countries which had sparse populations in relation to their available resources. Here we have an interesting situation which leads us straight into the fundamental issues of the development of the wage economy in the underdeveloped countries.

If we apply the ordinary demand and supply analysis to the labour market, we should expect to have a generally higher level of wages in sparsely populated countries than in densely populated countries. We should also expect the wage level to show a rising trend over a period of rapid expansion in output requiring more labour. These results are broadly borne out by experience in the newly settled regions of North America and Australia. But when we turn to the tropical underdeveloped countries which also started (in a lesser degree) with sparse populations in relation to the available land, these expected results failed to take place. Here the mine and plantation owners continually complained about 'labour shortage'. But the wages they paid in the sparsely populated countries were not noticeably higher than those they paid in the overpopulated countries. Moreover, these wages tended to stick at their initial level in spite of the rapid expansion in the production of the mining and plantation exports.

Origins of the 'cheap labour policy'

The owners of the mines and plantations usually explained this situation in terms of the very poor quality of labour they could recruit from the subsistence economies, whether densely or sparsely populated. According to them, the uniformly low level of wages which prevailed in all types of underdeveloped countries merely reflected the uniformly low level of labour productivity in all these countries. Some would go on to contrast the poor quality of indigenous labour with the better quality of the European immigrant labour which flowed into North America and Australasia, and use this to explain the pattern of high wages and high productivity which developed in these newly settled regions. Some would complain that even at the low wages paid, the indigenous labour was 'expensive' because its productivity was lower still.

To these quantitative and qualitative factors, I should add a third set of factors which affected the type of wage economy which developed in the underdeveloped countries. These factors include the employers' conventional beliefs that, in general, indigenous labour not only had low productivity but had limited capacity for improvement; and that it was used to the customarily low material standard of living and would not respond positively to the incentive of higher wages. This crystallized into the convention of maintaining low wages in the underdeveloped countries which may be contrasted with the convention of maintaining high wages in the newly settled regions. As we shall see, in the formative stages of the wage economy, these conventional standards of wages could play an important part in influencing the future path of development.

Let us now consider how these three sets of factors acted on each other. The comparative productivity of indigenous labour in the mining and plantation sector and in the peasant sector was affected in two ways. In so far as the mining and plantation sector employed modern methods of production using a larger amount of capital per unit of labour, we should expect the productivity of indigenous labour to be higher here than in the peasant sector. If this were the only effect, we should expect the mines and plantations to be able to attract labour from the peasant sector by paying higher wages based on higher productivity. But unfortunately, in the early stages of entry into the wage economy, the quality of the raw indigenous labour just emerging out of the subsistence economy was undoubtedly very poor. It was unused to the industrial discipline of having to work regularly and continuously at the new rhythm required by the productive organization of the mines and plantations. Frequently, it lacked basic physical stamina because of malnutrition and disease. It therefore needed some time before it could efficiently perform even the most unskilled of tasks, which confirmed the employers' beliefs about the limited capacity of indigenous labour. Now, given these handicaps of rawness and inexperience, the productivity of indigenous labour in the mining and plantation sector at the initial stage was not only below its potential long-term level; it was sometimes not much higher than its productivity in the peasant sector itself.

These transitional difficulties were not too serious in the overpopulated countries. Where the indigenous population was already struggling at the minimum subsistence level, the mines and plantations could obtain an adequate supply of labour even at the wage level fixed according to the low initial productivity of labour. But in the sparsely populated countries where peasant agriculture offered more attractive opportunities, the conflict between the quantitative and qualitative aspects of the labour supply gave rise to a dilemma with far-reaching consequences. (i) If the mines and plantations were to fix wages according to the initial short-run productivity of the raw labour, the wage level would be too low to attract a sufficient supply of labour and they would suffer from a 'labour shortage'. (ii) If they were to raise wages, and succeeded in attracting a sufficient supply of labour, they would suffer from having to pay the raw labour above its initial short-run productivity during the transition period. At this juncture, the third set of forces which I have described as the conventional standard of wages came into play, and the mines and plantations opted for the policy of keeping wages low.

The far-reaching consequences of this decision can be seen by contrasting the possible effects of the two alternatives. Had the mines and plantations adopted the policy of raising wages to attract more labour, the gap between the wages and the short-run productivity of the raw labour would have induced them to adopt various further policies of economizing labour and raising its productivity—say by more careful selection, gradation and training, or by the introduction of labour-saving methods such as a greater degree of mechanization. As we shall see, it would not have been easy to pursue such a policy in the setting of the underdeveloped countries, for there were further complications arising out of the transition phase itself. But if they had succeeded, then the mines and plantations would have performed their expected role as the 'leading sector', raising productivity in the rest of the economies in which they operated. As it was, their low wage policy induced them to use labour extravagantly, merely as an undifferentiated mass of 'cheap' or 'expendable' brawn-power. So through the vicious circle of low wages and low productivity, the productivity of the indigenous labour even in the sparsely populated countries was fossilized at its very low initial level.

At this point, it may be noted that the difference between the pattern of low wages and low productivity which developed in the thinly populated underdeveloped countries, and the pattern of high wages and high productivity which developed in the newly settled regions of North America and Australasia cannot be satisfactorily explained simply in terms of the better quality of the European immigrant labour in North America and Australasia. At a given moment of time, we may say that the high wages, say in the United States, were a reflection of the high productivity of labour. But over a period of time a rising trend in productivity can be achieved only if the employers can be induced to adopt labour-saving methods raising labour productivity. Here the importance of the conventional standard of high wages is that it creates a gap between wages and productivity, inducing employers to adopt labour-saving methods. Professor Taussig has pointed out that one of the reasons for the rapid development of mechanization and other labour-saving methods in American industry was the desire to maintain the high American wage level in the face of the *low* initial productivity of the fresh European immigrants who came into the country. This situation induced the invention of machinery 'that will almost run itself. Here the newly arrived immigrant can be used. So far as the American can do this sort of machine making to peculiar advantage, so far can he pay the immigrant on the higher American scale and yet hold his own against the European competitor who pays lower wages to the immigrant's stay-at-home fellow.'[1]

1. F. W. Taussig, *Some Aspects of the Tariff Question*, p. 43.

Migrant labour and the partial entry into the wage economy

Let us now turn to the question of how the mines and plantations managed to obtain any labour at all in the sparsely populated countries when the wages they offered were not very much above, or might even be below, the real income which the indigenous people could obtain in the subsistence economy. One very important factor which facilitated this was the 'migrant labour' system which still prevails in most of the mining and plantation economies of Africa. This again is a peculiarity of the transition stage. In the peasant sector, we have seen that at the early stage of entry into the money economy, the peasants produced the cash crop on a spare-time basis while continuing to produce their subsistence requirements. The migrant labour system is a counterpart of that, representing a partial entry into the wage economy. Under this system, those who came to work in the mines and plantations still retained a foothold in the subsistence economy. They regarded their wage-earning activity not as a permanent full-time employment but as a periodical spare-time activity to earn a certain sum of money *in addition* to their claims on the subsistence economy. They were therefore quite willing to accept the low wages offered by the mines and plantations since these were regarded not as full compensation for the alternative economic opportunities (which were not sacrificed) but merely as an additional source of income. But precisely because of this reason, the migrant labour normally returned to their families in the subsistence sector after having worked a certain period and having earned a certain target sum of money. They were then replaced by a fresh batch of recruits who in their turn worked and returned home.

In spite of its obvious short-term advantages, the migrant labour system reinforced the pattern of low wages and low productivity in a number of ways. With the high rate of labour turnover associated with the migrant labour system, it was not possible or worthwhile to select and train indigenous labour for skilled work, even if the mines and plantations were willing to do it. The same person did not stay on the job long enough for the purpose, and the labour supply remained a succession of raw recruits. But on the other hand, the migrant labour system provided the mines and plantations with a very convenient stream of casual labour for which they did not need to take much care and responsibility. Most of the workers were adult single males who had left (or were encouraged to leave) their families behind in the subsistence economy. So the mines and plantations did not feel obliged to pay wages sufficient to maintain the worker and his family or to invest in housing and other welfare projects to enable him to settle permanently with his family on the location of his work. Further, during the slumps in the export market, the redundant labour could be laid off and returned to the subsistence sector without continuing responsibility for them. We can now see why, having once started on the migrant labour system, the mines and plantations tried to perpetuate it as long as possible. The switch-over from a low-wage, low productivity pattern to a high-wage, high productivity pattern would involve not merely raising wages, but also the very heavy expenses and responsibilities of converting a casual labour force into a stabilized labour force on a permanent basis. One should also take into account the fact that investment flowed into the mines and plantations under the stimulus of shortages of their products and the high prices paid for them. They were therefore under continual pressure to take advantage of favourable market conditions which might change quickly. During the booms, therefore, output had to be expanded as quickly as possible along the line of least resistance, and there was no time to wait for the fruits of a longer term labour policy. During the slumps, no capital could be attracted to inaugurate such a policy.

The migrant labour system also strengthened the employers' belief that the indigenous people were not only content to accept low wages but did not respond positively to economic incentives. This was supposed to be 'proved' by the fact that the migrant workers who usually came to work to earn a fixed target sum of money (to meet their marriage expenses, for example) could be made to work for a longer period when the wage rate was reduced. But this reaction could also be induced from workers in the advanced countries provided the employers could press down the wage rate without restraint from the trade unions or public opinion. The real point, therefore, is whether the wants of the indigenous people were so limited that they would prefer not to earn above a certain sum; that is to say, whether the target sum they set out to earn was not merely a minimum but also a maximum target. Now, it may frequently happen that in the short run, given a sudden and transient rise in wage rates, the supply of indigenous labour would contract. But as we have seen from the behaviour of peasant producers, the indigenous people responded very vigorously to sustained positive economic incentives over the long period during which new wants and luxuries became semi-necessities. It is difficult, therefore, to accept this doctrine of the 'backward-bending' supply curve of labour in the underdeveloped countries without further evidence that a systematic application of wage incentives in favour of extra work, such as bonuses and overtime payments, had failed to induce a greater supply of labour over the long run.

Whatever its weaknesses, the doctrine of the 'backward-bending' supply curve of labour was used to rationalize the policy of using negative pressures to squeeze more labour out of the subsistence economy when the voluntary supply of migrant labour became inadequate for the expanding demand of the mines and plantations. Sometimes the pressure was applied directly, and the administrative power of the colonial government or indigenous rulers was used to direct labour into the mines and plantations. More frequently, the pressure was applied indirectly, by imposing a poll tax or a hut tax which obliged the indigenous people in the subsistence economy to come out and work in the mines and plantations so that they could pay their taxes.

These compulsive measures required the active co-operation of the colonial governments, and they had two chief motives in supporting this policy. First, the colonial governments needed money badly to finance their basic expenditure, including social and economic expenditure to stimulate development, and the royalties and taxation they could impose on the mines and plantations formed a very important, frequently their main, source of revenue. Secondly, many colonial governments were themselves large employers of indigenous labour for public works, transport and communications, and they were interested in keeping wages low. But this sponsoring of the cheap labour policy had far-reaching implications. Since peasant production was the main alternative to working for money wages, it followed that there was a conflict of interest between providing cheap labour for the mines and plantations and for the government, and the development of peasant cash production. In so far as the colonial governments regarded the requirement of cheap labour to be of paramount interest, therefore, peasant agriculture was deliberately discouraged or at least largely neglected so as not to spoil the labour market. There were, however, important exceptions to this pattern. The peasant export economies of Ghana and Nigeria were fostered by a deliberate policy of prohibiting plantation production of peasant crops, and in Uganda peasant production of cotton was allowed to prosper in spite of labour shortage for coffee plantations. Elsewhere, colonial administrators frequently discouraged peasant cash crops, not from sinister motives, but merely because they wished to reduce the chances of local famines—chances which could be increased by growing too much of the cash crops in remote areas where transport and communications were bad.

In most African countries the mines and plantations have so far been able to obtain the bulk of their labour requirements on the basis of the migrant labour system, reinforced by taxation and administrative pressures. With the economic power the mines and plantations have as monopolistic employers of labour, the pressure of expanding demand for labour and the alternative economic opportunities offered by peasant cash production have not been able to break the mould of the cheap labour policy. All that alternative economic opportunities can do is to regulate the supply of labour from different regions— regions with prosperous peasant agriculture sending relatively little labour, and regions with little or no peasant cash crops supplying the bulk of the labour for the mines and plantations.[1]

Immigrant labour

In other underdeveloped countries, such as Malaya and Ceylon, where migrant labour of the African type was not available on a sufficient scale, or where the development of peasant cash crops made taxation an ineffective method of increasing the supply of labour to the mines and plantations, a different solution was adopted. This was to import immigrant labour systematically and on a large scale from the overpopulated countries of India and China. The method of obtaining 'indentured' labour from India under which the employers agreed to

1. See the U.N. Report on the *Enlargement of the Exchange Economy*, cited above, Tables 9 and 10, and also W. J. Barber, *The Economy of British Central Africa*, Chs. 8 and 9.

pay the passage of the immigrant workers in return for an agreement to work a certain number of years for a certain wage rate was first adopted in the sugar plantations of the West Indies after the emancipation of the slave labour. After that, it spread not only to the countries of South-East Asia, but also to places such as Fiji, Mauritius, or East and Central Africa. Indeed, the immigrant labour from India and China was recruited on so large a scale that it has been said that these two countries, together with Britain, were the 'three mother countries' of the British Empire.[1]

Both migrant and immigrant labour involved movements of labour across national boundaries into the underdeveloped countries where the mines and plantations were located. The difference is that whereas the African type of migrant worker accepted the low wages offered by the mines and plantations as an addition to his income from the subsistence economy, the Indian and the Chinese immigrants accepted them because they could not find work even at these low wages in the overpopulated countries from which they came. In their case, however, the effect was to depress the wage level in the thinly populated underdeveloped countries to that of the overpopulated countries. Without appreciably relieving the population pressure in India and China, the outflow of cheap labour from these countries created serious problems for the underdeveloped countries which received it. In many of these countries, the Indian and Chinese labour came to form a considerable proportion of the total population, and frequently had a faster rate of growth than the indigenous population. When the indigenous population itself began to grow, therefore, the problem of population pressure was aggravated. Further, particularly in the South-East Asian countries, the presence of large Indian or Chinese minorities has created the complex socio-economic

1. L. C. Knowles, *The Economic Development of the British Overseas Empire*, vol. I, pp. viii and 182–201.

problems of the 'plural society' which frequently overshadow the problem of economic development itself.

Mines and plantations and economic development

In recent times, it has become fashionable to look upon the mines and plantations as 'foreign enclaves' which are incapable of transmitting a satisfactory type of economic growth to the developing countries. The critics tend to put most of the blame on the fact that they are concerned with primary production and not with manufacturing industry. Our analysis has, however, suggested that the failure of the mines and plantations to become the 'leading sector' in the underdeveloped countries was due, not to their producing primary exports as such, but to their cheap labour policy which has perpetuated the pattern of low wages and low productivity. With the system of using indigenous labour mainly as an undifferentiated mass of brawn-power, it is not surprising that Adam Smith's vision of the growth of the exchange economy and the division of labour 'improving the skill and dexterity of the people' should remain largely unfulfilled. The 'dualism' between foreign technology and management in the mines and plantations representing the 'modern' sector, and the rest of the economy representing the traditional sector has persisted.

If the mines and plantations did little to raise the technical efficiency of the indigenous people, how far have they extended the people's purely market opportunities? In many African mining economies, the existence of a large number of wage earners has created regular markets for staple food produced by indigenous cultivators.[1] The wage income from the mines

1. U.N. Report on the *Enlargement of the Exchange Economy*, pp. 32–3; Cf., however, W. J. Barber, op. cit., pp. 183–4 on the limitations on the market opportunities of the indigenous cultivators either because some plantations grow the food for their labour or because the mines purchase it from the European settler farmers.

and plantations has the same effect in spreading the money economy as the cash income from peasant production. But even here there is a snag. We have seen that the money economy cannot spread fully in the peasant sector until the peasants have switched over from part-time to full-time production of cash crops, buying their food requirements from other farmers. Similarly, the wages paid out by the mines and plantations cannot give rise to the full extent of secondary rounds of economic activity without further specialization. That is to say, the migrant labour force with one foot in the wage economy and another in the subsistence economy has to develop into two specialized groups, one consisting of a permanent stabilized body of full-time wage earners and the other specializing in full-time production of the cash crops. But while the peasant producer can assume full-time status by expanding his output while accepting the same market price per unit of his output, the migrant labourer cannot turn himself into a full-time wage employee so easily. His wages already represent full-time work during the short periods for which he has taken up employment. The total earnings required to support himself and his family after they have become 'detribalized' without any further claim on the subsistence economy can therefore be met only by raising the wage per unit of his labour. On the other hand, for the mines and plantations, this switch-over means not merely raising wage rates, but also incurring the very heavy expenses in housing and welfare projects, and all the responsibilities of turning a casual labour force into a stabilized labour force. Although some exceptionally prosperous mining regions such as the Copper Belt in Northern Rhodesia or the Belgian Congo may be prepared to do this, others have not been able to follow this example.[1]

1. W. J. Barber, op. cit., pp. 232–3, stated that the Northern Rhodesian mining industry spent more than £42 per worker in 1953 to stabilize the labour force and that this represented more than a 50% increase on the average annual income received in kind per worker in 1949.

E

How far can the mines and plantations contribute to the future growth of the developing economies? Here, as in the previous chapter, I shall defer consideration of the factors which may affect the future world market demand for these primary exports to Chapter 9 and concentrate on the points which have emerged so far from my analysis of the supply side of the question. It seems that in the context of many of the newly independent countries, the foreign-owned mines and plantations have been prevented from making their full potential contribution to economic development by two formidable obstacles.

The first is the wholesale reaction against primary production and in favour of manufacturing industries on the part of the governments of the newly independent countries, even where there is no serious population pressure and 'disguised unemployment'. The second is the rising tide of economic nationalism. We have already seen that the function of the marketing boards in the peasant export economies is not merely to stabilize prices but also to nationalize the foreign-owned export-import firms or reduce their profits. In the mining and plantation economies, the reaction against the past colonial pattern is even stronger, since economic nationalism is reinforced by the conventional conflict between indigenous labour and foreign capital. In extreme cases, there has been outright nationalization of all foreign-owned enterprises. More generally, there have been attempts to obtain a larger share of their profits through higher taxation and royalties, and a larger share of their management through requiring a larger number of indigenous personnel in the skilled and managerial grades. In addition, there have been attempts to improve wages and working conditions through government and trade union pressures, and through labour laws covering, for example, minimum wages, welfare and social security.

In so far as these measures help to break down the old

pattern of cheap labour policy and pave the way for raising the productivity of indigenous labour, they will contribute to economic growth. The question is how far these policies, which are primarily designed to get a larger share of the existing cake for the nationals of the underdeveloped countries, are compatible with the development policy of trying to increase the total size of the cake.

Fundamentally, the importance of trying to retain foreign enterprises in the developing countries is not only the capital they may bring in but also the technical skills and knowledge they have built up for long periods in the past in the context of the local conditions. Skills and knowledge, available in a well-articulated form and fitted into a going economic concern, are less easily replaceable than capital funds which may be obtainable from other sources. If properly tapped, therefore, their 'educative' effect on the countries concerned may be much greater than many of the technical aid programmes using a fresh group of 'foreign experts' who have no local knowledge. But the mines and plantations cannot function as the 'leading sector', diffusing modern technology and skills to the underdeveloped countries, unless they can switch over from their traditional cheap labour policy to a new pattern of higher wages and higher productivity. As we have seen, however, this requires heavy additional investments on their part both in material and human capital, and they are naturally unwilling to undertake these investments unless they can be reasonably sure of reaping the fruits in the long run. But unfortunately, in the typical conditions of the newly independent countries, this sense of security and inducement to wait for the fruits of a longer-term policy is precisely what is not available to the foreign-owned enterprises. In addition to the traditional insecurity created by the instability of prices in the world market, the mines and plantations now have to contend with additional sources of insecurity such as the further tightening of controls over their operations and remittances of profits, general political instability and the threat of nationalization. It is not so much the inherent limitation of primary export production as such, but lack of the conditions necessary for the pursuit of longer-term policies which seems to have prevented the foreign-owned mines and plantations from making their full potential contributions to the economic growth of the developing countries.

5

Financial Dualism and Monetary
Dependence and Independence

Capital supply in the peasant sector

In the subsistence economy, each social unit such as the family
or the village not only produces what it requires but also supplies its own productive resources, including capital. Saving
mainly takes the form of an addition to the 'subsistence fund',
enabling it to maintain a larger number of workers, or the same
number of workers for a longer time. Given this, investment in
durable capital can take place in various forms, such as the
clearing of additional land for cultivation, or the construction
of implements, irrigation works, public or private buildings.
As we have seen, in the first phase of the money economy, the
peasants produced the cash crop for export on a part-time
basis while continuing to produce their subsistence crop. The
expansion of peasant export production in this phase, therefore, was mainly 'self-financing'.

The spread of the money economy into the market for commodities and the improvement in transport and communications by themselves tend to economize the stocks of goods or
the 'subsistence fund' which an underdeveloped society needs
to carry itself on between one harvest and another. While each
family unit had previously to carry its own stocks for emergency, now the function of carrying them in a pool for a larger
number of family units is taken over by the village shop.
Similarly, the effect of the spread of trade and communications

in preventing local famines illustrates this economizing of reserve stocks of goods.

But the expansion of world demand for peasant exports required a quicker rate of new investment in the clearing of land than an individual family could usually finance out of its own savings and, with greater specialization, many families now switched over to a full-time production of the export crop, buying their food and other requirements. Even in this second stage, peasant producers could be self-financing provided they saved enough out of their proceeds from the cash crop. But in the majority of cases this did not happen, partly because of a high propensity to spend on imported goods and partly because of inexperience with a highly unstable export market which made peasant producers believe that the high prices of the good years would continue in the future. Lured by these optimistic expectations, they tended to borrow heavily to extend cultivation and to get into debt when prices came down.

Now the main source from which the peasants could borrow were and still are the 'non-institutional' lenders, such as the village money-lender, the landlord or the shopkeeper. The interest rates charged on these loans are usually very high.[1] The main reason for this is a real shortage of savings, but there are many important contributory factors arising out of imperfections in the market for borrowing and lending in the peasant sector. Considering the substantial amount of saving in this sector which still remains locked up in hoarded gold and jewellery, there seems to be scope for the introduction of a more efficient class of financial intermediaries which could bring down the interest rates to some extent. But so far little progress has

1. A recent study has estimated that they range on the average between 24% and 36% per annum. The institutional lenders such as the co-operative societies are still generally inadequate, although in some cases, such as in West Africa, big export-import firms give considerable advances to the peasants through produce buyers. (U. Tun Wai, Interest Rates Outside the Organised Money Markets; *I.M.F. Staff Papers*, November 1957.)

been made in this direction. The Western commercial banks have offered little competition to the money-lenders because these banks are, so to speak, wholesalers dealing with larger amounts of loan, whereas the peasants require an efficient retail distribution of credit. On the other hand, the money-lenders frequently occupy strategic positions in the local economy such as that of village shopkeeper or landlord and can so consolidate their monopoly powers over the peasants. The high rates of interest which the peasants have to pay are not only formal interest charges but also in considerable part concealed charges obtained through manipulating the prices of the commodities which the peasants buy or sell. Concealed charges may take the form of very high prices for goods on credit terms at the local shop or the obligation to repay the landlord the loans he advanced with a specified amount of the crop at harvest.

The financial 'dualism' between the organized and the unorganized money markets in the underdeveloped countries

The imperfections in the unorganized money market in the peasant sector offer a striking contrast with the low interest rates and abundant credit facilities available in the organized money market of the underdeveloped countries. Here the big foreign trading enterprises, mines and plantations, can raise their long-term capital at low rates of interest from the world capital markets. They can also borrow their short-term capital requirements cheaply from the commercial banks which are themselves branches of the banks located in the world financial centres. During the colonial period, one of the duties of the metropolitan power was to introduce the governments of the underdeveloped countries to the world capital market (a function now taken over by the World Bank). During that period, therefore, the governments also could raise their long-term capital cheaply from the world capital market. Apart from their imperial connection, one of the reasons why colonial governments in the pre-war days could usually borrow more cheaply than can the governments of the independent under-developed countries was the stability of the colonial type currency which precluded inflationary developments of the sort experienced by Japan and still being experienced in some of the Latin American countries.

The dualism we have seen between the peasant sector on the one hand and the plantation and mining sector on the other, with respect to economic organization and production methods, is paralleled by the financial dualism between the two sectors. Considering the high rates of interest and the small amount of capital used per unit of labour and per unit of output in the peasant sector, and contrasting them with the low rates of interest and the capital intensive methods of production in the mining and plantation sector, it is tempting to argue that the total available capital resources have been misallocated between the two sectors, and that total output would be increased by diverting a part of the capital supply from the mining and plantation sector to the peasant sector. This is, however, too mechanical an application of a familiar economic theorem which assumes that a homogeneous economy can freely allocate its capital supply to alternative uses without thereby affecting the total amount of capital available to it. This is not true, however, in the dualistic setting of an underdeveloped country. Here, private foreign capital flowed into the country for the specific purpose of investment in the mining and plantation sector in response to favourable world market prices for particular commodities which that sector could produce. In other words, there was no choice of re-allocating the inflow of foreign private capital between the peasant sector and the plantation and mining sector according to the optimum theory. The only available choice was having private investment in the mining and plantation sector or not having any private foreign investment at all.

This cuts across some of the familiar arguments for and against the colonial economic pattern. It will be seen that the critics were not on strong ground when they blamed the colonial governments for encouraging foreign investment only in primary production without attracting a part of it to domestic manufacturing industry. The governments had really very little choice in the matter. In any case, the size of the domestic markets for manufactured goods in the underdeveloped countries was generally too small to attract private foreign capital into domestic manufacturing industry. But the advantages which the people of the colonial countries obtained from the great financial centres in the metropolitan countries should not be exaggerated. Directly, in their role as peasants, small traders, handicraft producers, they obtained little or no benefit from it. Only indirectly, mainly through government investment in transport and communications and other public work, could they count their benefits.

Two more points can be made. First, the Western commercial banks which operate in the underdeveloped countries not only concentrate too much on the export sector as against the domestic sector, but also tend to adopt rigid and conservative rules of credit-worthiness which few even of the bigger indigenous borrowers in the export sector can hope to satisfy, so giving some substance to the complaint that they discriminate against the indigenous businessman.[1] Moreover, with their lending policy of concentrating on short-term loans to big foreign enterprises in the export sector, their operations frequently result in 'perverse' flows of credit. That is to say, instead of channelling the funds from the world financial centres to the underdeveloped countries, they are frequently instrumental in lending some part of the local savings they have collected in the

1. P. T. Bauer, *West African Trade*, Ch. 13, section 5.

underdeveloped countries to the world financial centres. For instance, it has been estimated that between 1954 and 1959, some 20% to 30% of the funds collected by the banks in the British colonial territories have been remitted out of these territories, almost wholly to the London head offices or money market.[1]

Secondly, even in terms of the total flow of foreign capital to the underdeveloped countries, the share of the nineteenth-century foreign investment which flowed into the present-day underdeveloped countries was much smaller than is generally imagined. The bulk of it went elsewhere to the newly settled regions of North America and Australasia, to the Western European countries at the early stages of industrial development and to exceptionally large countries like Russia, China and India offering scope for railway investment. As Professor Cairncross has pointed out: 'it is unlikely that the less advanced countries as a group obtained more than $500m a year in foreign investment in the decade before 1914 when the international flow of capital was at its tide'. He contrasts this with the current rate of capital transfer including aid to these countries which exceeded $5 billion a year by 1958-9.[2]

1. E. Nevin, op. cit., pp. 50-1. In doing this because there are insufficient local investment opportunities sound enough by their rules, the banks are of course protecting their depositors' interests for securing absolute safety for their money. Here the depositors' preference for absolute safety of their assets is essentially the same type of reaction as the peasants' hoarding of his savings in the form of gold and jewellery to hedge against inflation. How far an underdeveloped country short of capital should allow individuals to satisfy their high preference for riskless assets is a delicate matter. When we take into account the long-term effect on thrift and development of modern monetary institutions, the balance of considerations may not always lie with those who wish to 'mobilize' all these idle assets ruthlessly.

2. A. K. Cairncross, *Factors in Economic Development*, pp. 41 and 55.

The dependent monetary system

Until recently the monetary system which prevailed in most Asian and African countries was a colonial type of monetary system, typified by the sterling exchange standard. Under this system, the currency of a colony was freely convertible at a fixed rate of exchange with sterling. It was issued by a currency board located in London and the issue was generally backed by 100% sterling reserves contributed out of the export earnings of the colony. The currency board was required to invest its reserve fund outside the colony, in British or other Commonwealth Government securities, although the colony received its share of the currency board profits. In effect, the colony was obliged to lend its monetary reserve funds to other countries in the Commonwealth. In line with the general reaction against the colonial economic pattern, this system has been criticized as being too rigid to provide adequately for the financial requirements of a developing country. I shall therefore briefly outline its working and contrast it later with the working of an independent monetary system.

The working of the 100% sterling exchange system in its pure form may be illustrated in terms of my model of the two stages in the growth of the money economy in a peasant export economy. In the first stage, the peasants produced the export crop only on a part-time basis while continuing to produce their subsistence requirements. Since they were self-sufficient in respect to locally produced foodstuffs and other goods, they had no need to hold cash for local transactions. Since their sole reason for producing the export crop was to obtain purchasing power over imports, we may assume that they spent the whole of their cash earnings on imported goods. At this stage, the money which flowed into the country to pay for the peasants' exports would flow out again immediately to pay for their imports. No 'localized' currency would be retained for long within the country. The function of money was merely to facilitate the barter between the exports and imports at agreed rates and a separate local currency was hardly needed. As a matter of fact, in the earlier phases of trade in West Africa, British silver coins were extensively used for this purpose.

In the second stage, the money economy has spread from foreign trade to domestic trade. Some of the peasants now devote all their resources to export production and no longer produce their subsistence requirements of foodstuffs and local commodities. So instead of spending the whole of their money income on imports only, they will spend a part of it on locally produced goods and services. What is more, since money transactions have now become more frequent, they will need to hold a certain amount of cash for carrying on their normal transactions.

They may also save and hoard money as a store of value for future needs. Similarly, those who receive the money payments from export producers in subsequent rounds of buying and selling will spend a part of their income on imports and a part of it on locally produced goods. They will also hold a certain amount of cash for normal transactions and saving. So of the total amount of money which has flowed into the country to pay for the peasants' exports, the part which has not flowed out again to pay for the imported goods purchased by the peasant exporters and by all those who receive money payments from them will be retained inside the country as 'localized' currency. The amount of the localized currency is equal to the peasant producers' total earnings from export minus total spending on imports by themselves and all others who receive money payments from them. This surplus of earnings over expenditure by the residents of the country in terms of the foreign currency contributes to the 100% sterling reserve for the localized currency. This result follows because the country in my example has no other means of acquiring its supply of money except through its exports.

I have said that the amount of the localized currency is equal to 'the surplus of earnings over expenditure in terms of the foreign currency by the residents of the country' and have used this clumsy phrase deliberately to distinguish it from the geographical export surplus in the usual sense as shown by the trade figures. In my example, even if the country has no other source of exports than the peasant exports, the geographical export surplus will be different from the relevant surplus in our sense. For the geographical export surplus will include payments to the non-residents such as the profit remittances of the foreign export-import firms. What is relevant for our present purpose is the surplus earning of foreign exchange accruing to the residents of the country; they could have imported consumers' or capital goods but have preferred to pass it on to the currency board because they wish to hold their assets in the form of local currency.

I can now easily extend the analysis to determine the amount of the localized currency for a more general type of economy whose exports originate not only from the peasant sector but also from the plantation and mining sector. In this case the export earners will include not only peasant producers but all other resident wage earners in the mines and plantations and other auxiliary export industries such as transport and processing. We should also remember that the amount of localized currency existing at a given time within a country is an accumulated stock; the surplus foreign exchange earnings of the residents each year add to the stock and the deficit foreign exchange expenditure of the residents subtract from it.

I can now introduce two qualifications into my simplified account of the 100% sterling exchange system. In recent years, varying proportions of a country's currency reserve have been permitted to be invested in that country's own government securities. In Jamaica, the currency authorities could hold as much as one-third of their reserves in local securities by the end of 1959, although for the colonial territories as a group over 80% of their currency reserve funds was still held in London.[1] The second qualification is of course the operation of commercial banks which can create deposits many times larger than their cash reserves in local currency and can therefore cut the rigid connection between a country's surplus foreign exchange earnings and the additional supply of its local currency. However, commercial banking has two limitations in underdeveloped countries. First, in many of these countries banking habits have not developed and the ratio of bank deposit money to the total money supply is lower than in the advanced countries. However, this ratio has been steadily increasing, say to about 30% or 40% of the total supply of money in the 1950s for many Asian countries (and somewhat higher ratios for the Latin American countries) compared with a ratio ranging between 60% and 80% for the advanced countries.[2] Secondly, as we have seen, in many British colonial or Commonwealth countries, the banks which operated until recent times were branches of the big London banks, mainly interested in short-term lending to the foreign enterprises in the export industries. So the peasant producers and other smaller borrowers in domestic trade and industry have not derived much benefit from the 'elasticity' which the commercial banks can impart to the local money supply.

Monetary independence

In the recent post-war years, with the attainment of political independence, the developing countries of Asia and Africa

1. E. Nevin, *Capital Funds in Underdeveloped Countries*, pp. 7–8.
2. U Tun Wai, loc. cit., *I.M.F. Staff Papers*, August 1956, p. 251.

have also asserted their monetary independence by establishing their own central banks. The Latin American countries did this in the 1920s or 1930s, and India and Thailand also have central banks dating from that period. The external limit to the currency issue is removed and the governments of these countries can now borrow from the central banks to meet their budget deficits. The newly established central banks, however, do not have the power, which their counterparts in the advanced countries have, to control the commercial banks through traditional methods such as changing the central bank rate or varying the supply of money by buying or selling securities in the open market. For one thing, the stock exchange and the money market in these countries are too underdeveloped for this purpose. For another, the foreign commercial banks look upon their headquarters in London or elsewhere and not upon the local central bank as their 'lender of the last resort'. To make up for this, the central banks in many countries have been granted extensive legal powers (which have not so far been fully exercised) over the commercial banks, ranging from requirements to hold certain minimum proportions of their funds with the central banks, to more detailed controls over their rates of interest, the amount and direction of their lending and other 'selective controls'.[1] Finally, in addition to the central banks, many government 'development banks' have been set up to finance domestic industry and agriculture.

How far do these changes help the economic development of these countries in so far as it can be influenced by monetary and financial factors?

Under the old sterling exchange type of monetary system, inflation was avoided by a control over the currency issue combined with the tradition of a balanced budget. Further, the automatic convertibility between the local currency and sterling

1. U Tun Wai, loc. cit., *I.M.F. Staff Papers*, August 1956, pp. 258–62; E. Nevin, op. cit., Ch. 2; and A. K. Cairncross, op. cit., Ch. 10.

eliminated balance of payments disequilibrium. Thus when a country had an excess of imports over exports, an equivalent amount of local currency was converted into sterling to pay for the deficit, and the reduction of the local money supply reduced the incomes until imports were equated to exports at a lower equilibrium level. With the attainment of monetary independence, however, most of the developing countries have suffered from varying degrees of inflation, and some of the more extreme cases are to be found in Latin America. Further, owing to various factors such as the decline in foreign exchange reserves, balance of payments pressure and a general decline in confidence aggravated in many cases by political instability, the external values of the currencies of the developing countries have generally fallen below the official rates of exchange, setting up pressures for one-way conversion of the local currency into a more stable international currency. The developing countries are, however, unwilling to lower their official rates of exchange to the free market level, either because they wish to avoid a worsening in the terms of trade between their exports and their imports or because they fear that, once they start devaluing their currency, they may be caught up in a cumulative spiral of inflation and devaluation. They have, therefore, concentrated mainly on tightening their controls on foreign exchange and imports, using quantitative controls of varying complexity and severeness.

Some of the critics of the old monetary system have argued that while monetary stability was indispensable in the days when economic development was left to foreign private enterprise, it is no longer of vital importance at the present time. The governments of the developing countries have taken over the function of economic development, and an increasing amount of external capital flows through international or intergovernmental channels. While this argument has considerable force, it tends to underrate the consequences of monetary instability on the domestic private sector of the underdeveloped countries. It should be remembered that many underdeveloped countries, notably in Africa, are still in the early stages of development of the money economy, with the larger part of their productive resources in the subsistence sector. Further, in almost all underdeveloped countries, the exchange economy has yet to spread from the market for commodities to the market for factors of production, particularly towards a more developed wage economy and capital market. This, however, requires not merely a wider use of money as a medium of exchange, but also developing the habit of using money as a 'unit of account' for more rational allocation of resources, and what is more important for our present purpose, using money as a 'store of value' for economic assets. On the other hand, with monetary policies which induce a distrust in the use of money as a unit of account and a flight from money as a store of value, it is difficult to see how the domestic resources of the underdeveloped countries can be effectively mobilized by a more comprehensive growth of the money economy. Similarly, it is a little one-sided to assume that the stability of the external value of the currency of an underdeveloped country and the absence of import controls mainly benefit foreign investors and foreign enterprises and not the indigenous people. After all, the high ratio of export to the national income in these countries also means a high import ratio and a widespread dependence on imports. In some of the African peasant economies in the earlier stage of development, imports may still have to play their role as incentive goods for expanding export production and the money economy. Elsewhere, domestic private industries have come to depend on imported producers' goods and it is not unknown for many infant industries of the underdeveloped countries to be stifled by the difficulties and delays of obtaining import licences for essential raw materials, capital equipment and spare parts.

F

Against these disadvantages, there are three possible advantages from having an independent monetary system.

First, under the old system the fluctuations in incomes of the underdeveloped countries caused by the export booms and slumps tended to be magnified through the free operation of commercial banks. Commercial banks tend to expand credit during the booms because their cash reserves have increased, and contract lending during the slumps, aggravating the fall in incomes. So, in theory at least, there is a good case for the central bank to pursue a contra-cyclical policy of moderating the expansion in incomes during the boom and adding to its foreign exchange reserves, and moderating the fall in income during the slump and releasing foreign exchange to pay for the excess imports which would follow from such a policy. But, in practice, this can be done only if the central bank can stock up foreign exchange during a boom. Unfortunately, with the upward surge of government expenditure during a boom (such as the Korean boom), the central bank has not usually been able to accumulate enough foreign exchange reserves to pursue such a policy.

Secondly, now that the central bank can increase the supply of money without having to acquire an equivalent amount of foreign exchange, and without having to invest a large part of it outside the country, it may be able to release some funds for domestic long-term investment out of its currency reserves. When the central bank first took over the reserves from the currency board, the release of funds for this purpose was sometimes quite substantial, but it was a once-for-all transfer. How far the central bank can release funds for domestic investment on a continuing basis depends on how seriously it takes its duty of maintaining the external value of the currency. If, for instance, it wishes to achieve the same degree of stability of the external value of the currency as under the old system, it cannot hope to economize its reserves very much to release funds for other purposes. One of the hard facts of life is that the external world tends to have more confidence, other things being equal, in a national currency which is freely convertible into a well-established international currency than in one which is not convertible.

The third possible advantage which may be claimed for an independent monetary system is of course that of deficit financing for economic development. I shall have more to say about this subject later on, in Chapter 8; for the moment only one point need be made. Deficit financing was originally advocated to deal with a situation of depression in the advanced countries. Now this situation differs from that of the underdeveloped countries in that in the advanced countries both unemployed labour and all the productive capacity which goes with it are readily available and can be made to increase output in a short time. By contrast, in the underdeveloped countries we either have unemployed labour without other productive resources, as in the overpopulated countries, or underutilized land, labour and savings which are the result of market imperfections, incomplete growth of the exchange economy and other *structural* defects of the economic system. Unlike the unemployed resources of the advanced countries in a depression, the potentially available resources of the underdeveloped countries have to be mobilized over a long period, mainly by correcting the structural defects which have given rise to them. The level of output in the advanced countries in a depression can be raised by expanding the aggregate amount of effective demand, but the expansion of output in the underdeveloped countries depends more on the way in which the extra funds are injected into particular parts of the economy than merely on the aggregate amount of funds that deficit financing creates.

We have already seen examples of the structural defects in the underdeveloped countries in the form of the 'dualism' in economic organization, technology and financing between the indigenous sector made up of peasants and other small-scale producers, and the modern sector made up of larger foreign enterprises and the government. If we wish to assess how far the recent changes in the monetary and banking systems of the developing countries have helped to improve the financing of investment, we shall have to look not so much at the ability of the central bank to increase the aggregate supply of money as at its ability to direct the activities of the private commercial banks and the government development banks towards a more effective development of indigenous trade, industry and peasant agriculture. Neither the commercial banks nor the government development banks have progressed very far in meeting the problems of financial dualism, although to be fair it must be admitted that the problems are intractable and require a much longer time than they have had so far.

6

Population Pressure and Aggregate Capital Requirements

The major driving force behind the study of the underdeveloped countries in the post-war years has been the desire to show that something should be done urgently to relieve their poverty. It is not difficult to understand, therefore, why the case of the overpopulated countries should come to be adopted as the prototype for all underdeveloped countries. With their acute material poverty, it is difficult at first sight to imagine how the overpopulated countries can increase their savings without grave hardships. On the other hand, their surplus population on the land seems to offer a major unused potential for economic development, waiting only for the 'missing component' of outside capital to assist them in the process. Moreover, their rapid rates of population growth lend themselves to calculations of aggregate capital requirements which must be made available if their per capita incomes are to be maintained or raised to a level determined by humanitarian considerations. All in all, the drama of the poor countries struggling at the minimum subsistence level and the need for a massive dose of outside capital to break the interlocking vicious circles which hold them down to that level does not attain its full tragic grandeur unless viewed against the background of overpopulation.

In this chapter I shall examine the two leading ideas which have dominated the writings on this subject, particularly in the early 1950s—the concept of 'disguised unemployment', and the general proposition that all underdeveloped countries need to save and invest not less than 10% of their aggregate national income to achieve economic development.

'Disguised unemployment' and underemployment

The concept of 'disguised unemployment' is not so widely accepted as it used to be about ten years ago. The argument popular at that time may be summarized as follows. In the overpopulated countries with extreme overcrowding on land, the marginal product of labour in agriculture is zero; a considerable amount of rural surplus labour can therefore be removed without reducing total agricultural output and can be put to use in the construction of productive capital goods, such as road and irrigation works. Since total agricultural output is not reduced by the removal of surplus labour, there will be more food left for those remaining on the land, and a food surplus can be extracted without reducing the per capita consumption of those who remain behind. This food surplus can then be used to feed those engaged in productive construction work. 'Disguised unemployment' therefore provides 'concealed savings' which can be used to build productive capital goods in a 'costless' way, and this without any fundamental improvements in agricultural techniques.

The chief conceptual weakness of 'disguised unemployment' arises from a failure to distinguish clearly between the zero marginal product of a unit of labour and the zero marginal product of a worker. This can be seen by taking a simple arithmetical example. Suppose that when 30 hours of work is put into a family holding, the marginal product of the 30th hour falls to zero. Assume that there are 6 workers in the family, sharing the work and output equally, so that each has to work 5 hours a day. Now with given agricultural techniques, the total output of the farm will remain unchanged as successive workers are removed, provided that the remaining workers work harder and longer to make up the total of 30 hours a day.

The first point which emerges is that there is nothing wrong with applying labour to land until the marginal product of the 30th hour of work falls to zero. Since no wages are paid and labour is free within the family, it will in fact be wasteful not to squeeze the most out of the scarce factor, land, until the marginal product of the abundant factor, labour, falls to zero. The possible waste in this situation arises not because the marginal product of the 30th hour of labour falls to zero, but because by working only 5 hours of the day, each of the 6 members of the family may be underemployed. The amount of 'disguised unemployment' depends on what we consider to be a full day's work for each. If we consider this to be 6 hours a day, there is disguised unemployment of one worker; if $7\frac{1}{2}$ hours a day, there is disguised unemployment of 2 workers; and if 10 hours a day, there is disguised unemployment of 3 workers.

Now the assumption that agricultural techniques remain unchanged merely means that the total output of the farm will remain unchanged so long as the total of 30 hours' work a day is performed. But in order to make those who remain on the land work harder to make up this total, there will have to be a considerable amount of reorganization, and provision of economic incentives. It should be noted that the number of hours which should be regarded as a 'full day's work' for those who remain behind is not unalterable. Depending on how efficiently the work is reorganized and how much economic incentives are offered, they may be induced to work 10 hours a day, making it possible to release 3 workers without reduction in total output; or $7\frac{1}{2}$ hours a day, releasing 2 workers; and so on. In the extreme case, where those who remain behind can obtain their minimum subsistence living by working only 5 hours each as before, and where no economic incentives are offered to induce them to work harder, it may not be possible to re-move 'disguised unemployment' without some reduction in agricultural output.

This creates serious difficulties for the argument that the social cost of using disguised unemployment is zero. If we rely on positive economic incentives to induce those who remain on the land to work harder, then they would have to be pro-vided with manufactured consumers' goods in exchange for their food surplus. The extra resources required for the produc-tion of these incentive consumers' goods constitute the social cost of keeping the agricultural output unchanged after the removal of disguised unemployment. If the proposal is to tax away the food surplus so that those who remain behind on the land cannot increase their per capita consumption, these forcible methods may work in the short run; but in the long run, there is likely to be a decline in agricultural output. It is very important to stress at this point that the problem of econ-omic development cannot be solved simply by a once-for-all transfer of food surplus from the peasants to the government in a given year. A continuous and sustained process is required, in which the *growing* food surplus from the agricultural sector is made available to feed a growing number of non-agricultural workers. This is more likely to be achieved by encouraging the peasants into the money economy by positive incentives rather than forcible measures which may drive them further back into the subsistence economy. Moreover, economic incentives should be regarded not merely as the method of inducing the peasants to sell the food surplus obtained with their existing agricultural techniques ,but more importantly as a method of inducing them to adopt better methods of production which will raise the food surplus in future.

Again, we may question the 'costless' nature of using 'disguised unemployment' when we turn to those who are removed from the land. It is now increasingly recognized that

creating employment for them would not only require additional investment in the form of housing and equipment but
would also generate extra consumption out of the new expanding wage incomes, adding to the total consumption of the community.[1] In a country like India, the social cost created by this
extra consumption is very concretely felt in the form of
serious pressures on limited food supplies. Thus even if the use
of 'disguised unemployment' did not reduce the total food
supply, it would add to the total demand for food. And the
creation of employment to absorb 'disguised unemployment'
can be justified only if its extra output in the new occupations
is large enough to cover the extra consumption which is gener-
ated. But the capital projects such as irrigation works and
roads in which 'disguised unemployment' is to be used do
not yield an immediately consumable output. We are then
led to the problems of the social cost of waiting in relation
to the size of the future income which will be considered in
Chapter 8.

'Disguised unemployment' is not confined to agriculture. In
many countries it is also to be found in varying degrees in the
towns and in non-agricultural occupations such as petty
trading, 'service industries' of all sorts including domestic
service, and in small scale and cottage industries. Here it is
caused by overcrowding on a limited supply of capital resources and productive equipment. It has been estimated, for
instance, that in India only a tiny proportion of the total working force, about 2%, are fully employed in the genuinely
modern industrial sector.[2] Outside this, 'disguised unemployment' pervades the whole economy in varying degrees. The
removal of 'disguised unemployment' from these non-agricultural occupations does not even leave a notional food surplus
to be mobilized. Further, the number of hours of 'work' in

1. A. K. Sen, *Choice of Techniques*, Ch. 5.
2. W. B. Reddaway, *The Development of the Indian Economy*, pp. 23–5.

these underemployed occupations are neither accurately measurable nor are very important, since, unlike what happens in the advanced countries, output per hour is so low that the wastage through underemployment is not likely to be very great. The essential problem, therefore, is, how to raise productivity and how to transfer labour from less to more productive work, irrespective of whether it is agricultural or non-agricultural.

The popular appeal of the 'disguised unemployment' arises from its claim to offer something for nothing in the way of a major potential for economic development. But unfortunately, as we shall increasingly see, the something for nothing principle rarely works except in limited cases. We can, for instance, think of using 'disguised unemployment' successfully in small-scale voluntary local construction works such as those sponsored by the community development projects. Beyond these limited cases, choices between the benefits and the costs have to be faced. Lured on by the something-for-nothing principle, however, the exponents have directed their attention to the wrong thing. Instead of concentrating on how to raise productivity, they have concentrated on how to increase the mere volume of unskilled work by extracting the surplus labour from agriculture, and have made a great point of saying that this can be done without improving the techniques of production. As we shall see, economic development is likely to be more effectively promoted by mobilizing the brain-power rather than the brawn-power of the people of the underdeveloped countries.

Aggregate capital requirements and the capital-output ratio

With the idea of capital as the 'missing component' of economic development which prevailed in the earlier post-war period, it was natural that economists should try to make estimates of the aggregate capital requirements of the developing countries, globally[1] and for each individual country. The most influential formula for an individual developing country was that it should save and invest not less than 10% to 12% of its national income. This was one of the three conditions for the 'take-off' laid down by Professor W. W. Rostow, and Professor W. A. Lewis put forward his well-known dictum that 'the central problem in the theory of economic growth is to understand the process by which a community is converted from being a 5 per cent to a 12 per cent saver—with all the changes in attitudes, in institutions and in techniques which accompany this conversion'.[2]

What was not clearly explained was that this formula can be arrived at in two significantly different ways. Professor Rostow's argument is based mainly on the historical analogy with the advanced countries in their take-off phase in the past, during which they had not only saved and invested more than 10% of their national income but, what is more important, *held on* to this high rate of saving and investment for two or three decades. It is a part of the intense economic effort which a developing country should make to launch itself into the take-off process which involves sharp and *discontinuous* changes in the production structure. On the other hand, the formula may also be arrived at by using the *stable* overall capital-output ratio on the Harrod–Domar growth model designed for the later 'mature' phase of the advanced countries after they have taken-off into steady growth. If the population of an underdeveloped country is growing at 2% per annum, its total national income must also be growing at 2% per annum to maintain its per capita income at the same level. If it is further desired that on humanitarian or political grounds, the

1. For the earliest and most well-known example of global calculations see United Nations Report on *Measures for Economic Development of Underdeveloped Countries*, 1951, Ch. 11, Table 2.

2. W. A. Lewis, *Theory of Economic Growth*, pp. 225–6.

per capita income itself should be raised by 2% per annum, then the total national income of the country should be growing approximately at 4% per annum. Now assume that in order to obtain an extra £1 worth of income the country requires to make an investment of £3, averaging out the different capital requirements between the different sectors of the economy—that is to say, its overall incremental capital-output ratio is 3. In order to raise the per capita income at the target rate of 2% per annum, requiring a 4% rate of increase in total income to take into account population increase, the country should be saving and investing $3 \times 4\% = 12\%$ of its national income each year.

Many writers have urged the developing countries to save and invest not less than 10% to 12% of the national income without explaining whether they are giving this advice (i) on the basis of the take-off theory implying sharp discontinuous changes in the production structure, or (ii) on the basis of a stable capital-output ratio implying a process of continuous steady economic growth. They shift freely between these two approaches, ignoring the fact that the 'take-off' phase (i) is separated by many decades of development from the 'mature' phase (ii). Nor have they been troubled by the fact that neither (i) nor (ii) might be applicable to many of the underdeveloped countries which are still at the earlier 'pre-take-off' stage.

(i) After our analysis of the earlier stages of the development of the money and the wage economy, we should now have a clearer appreciation of the fact that the underdeveloped countries are at very different stages of general economic development. A few of the relatively more advanced among them, such as India, Mexico or Brazil, may be somewhere within striking distance of the 'take-off' phase. But many more of them are still in the various stages of building their runway for the take-off. In particular, they lack the basic political, 'social and institutional framework' which both Professor Rostow and Professor Lewis would regard as the essential preconditions of the take-off. For instance, some of the underdeveloped countries are not yet able to maintain efficient law and order, whereas Professor Cairncross has reminded us, 'most countries that have staged a successful take-off have enjoyed an antecedent period of domestic peace which prevented the periodical destruction of physical assets and gave security to investment'.[1] Further, one of the less clearly appreciated aspects of Professor Rostow's theory is that, according to the historical examples he has given, a successful take-off requires not merely raising the saving and investment ratio above 10% of national income but maintaining it at that level for two or three decades. This requires a much higher ability not only to mobilize saving but also to invest it more effectively than the underdeveloped countries with their weak administrative, fiscal and monetary framework can be expected to have. Some of them with a high ratio of export to national income have been able to raise their saving ratio to the 10% level for a time during export booms, mainly by taxing the foreign trade sector which is easier to tax than the domestic sector. But they have not been able to sustain the process, and a considerable part of their windfall gains tends to be frittered away in inflation or prestige projects.

This, of course, does not mean that because countries are at the earlier stages of general development, they should not try to increase their rate of saving and investment. There are obvious fields: improvements in transport and communications alone can absorb a great deal of capital, both foreign and domestic. Again there are the 'pre-investments' in health, education, training and research, designed to increase 'human capital' and improve the country's capacity to absorb further investment. But nevertheless it is important to recognize that a country's progress towards economic development cannot be

1. A. K. Cairncross, *Factors in Economic Development*, p. 120.

judged simply by an overall ratio of saving and investment to national income without taking into account the qualitative and less easily measurable factors such as the efficiency and honesty of its administration, the degree of its political and monetary stability, or the skills and attitudes of the people. Nor is it wise to apply a mechanical rule-of-thumb which only represents one aspect of the take-off theory to all the underdeveloped countries at different stages of the pre-take-off period.

(ii) One obvious objection which can be made to the method of calculating the aggregate capital requirements of the underdeveloped countries on the basis of a stable overall capital-output ratio is that this implies the assumption of constant returns to scale for the expansion of the economy as a whole. This assumption is justified for the mature phase of the advanced countries to which the Harrod–Domar growth model is intended to apply. For these countries, primary production, which is subject to diminishing returns, forms a small part of their total output. Besides, technical progress and economies of scale are 'built in' to their economic life so that we can expect the forces for increasing returns to counteract the forces for diminishing returns. This is in fact confirmed by the advanced countries' experience of a steady and self-sustained process of economic growth for many decades. In contrast, one of the most well-established propositions about the underdeveloped countries is that agriculture and primary production forms the larger part of their national outputs and that *given unchanged techniques* the pressure of population increase on their given natural resources will result in conditions of diminishing returns to scale for the expansion of the economy as a whole.

This is as old as the Ricardian theory of the stationary state. It will be remembered that in the Ricardian theory, investment is looked upon not as the addition to the durable capital equipment, but mainly as the addition to the wage-fund or the sub-sistence-fund to be used to maintain a larger number of workers. The rate of profit on investment is measured by the difference between the marginal product of labour in agriculture and its wage rate (both measured in terms of the 'corn' or the general subsistence fund). As investment increases and more workers are put to work on the land, with given techniques the marginal product of labour will fall until it is equal to its wages. At this point, the rate of profit on investment falls to zero. This tend-ency to a declining rate of profit in agriculture is transmitted to the rest of the economy, particularly to the manufacturing sector, in the following way. Because of diminishing returns the rate of expansion in the agricultural output tends to lag behind that of the manufactured goods. This will raise the price of foodstuffs and raw materials in relation to the price of manu-factured goods, and so raise the cost of living for the workers employed in the manufacturing sector. In order to maintain the same real wage level, therefore, their money wages will have to be raised proportionately to the rise in price of subsistence goods and this will lead to a decline in the rate of profit on investment in the manufacturing sector. Once the general rate of profits has fallen to zero, there will be no further incentive to increase investment and the economy approaches the station-ary equilibrium.

In the language of the balanced growth theory (see Chapter 8) the Ricardian stationary state is brought about by the failure to expand the agricultural sector in a 'balanced growth' relation with the manufacturing sector, turning the inter-sectoral 'terms of trade' against the manufacturing sector. In the language of the capital-output ratio approach this means that diminishing returns which raise the cost of food for labour which enters into the production of the intermediate goods and capital goods will result in an increasing overall capital-output ratio as the economy expands. That is to say, we cannot apply the assumption of a stable overall capital-output ratio to the underdeveloped countries unless we can show at the same time how to counteract the general tendency towards diminishing returns. This becomes even more important when we remember that in many of these countries diminishing returns is not merely a matter of an increasing population pressing on a *given* amount of natural resources; the total available amount of natural resources is itself progressively reduced over time, because of overutilization and depletion through soil erosion, deforestation, or lowering of water tables, for example, not to mention the normal using up process of the mineral resources. In the language of the growth models, the assumption of a stable overall capital-output ratio for the underdeveloped countries requires not only that a continual stream of innovations is taking place, but that they are of a land-saving character, enabling a progressive substitution of capital and labour for natural resources.

In spite of this objection, the concept of an overall capital-output ratio has enjoyed a considerable vogue and it is frequently defended on the ground that it offers a useful basis for testing the consistency of the desired target rate of growth in national income and the available resources of a developing country. But in practice, we cannot get very far in testing the economic development plans of a country unless we are prepared to go behind the overall ratio into the structural factors which determine it.

The national income or output is not a homogeneous thing but is made up of different goods and services, each having widely varying capital-output ratios. The sectoral capital-output ratios are very high for some items, notably transport and communications and public utilities. Next in order of high capital-output ratios come housing and capital-goods industries. Manufactured consumers' goods industries together with other distributive and service industries generally have lower capital-output ratios.[1] The capital-output ratio in the agricultural sector of the underdeveloped countries is generally likely to be low, although some of the big irrigation and river valley projects require vast sums of capital. Characteristically, the expansion of agricultural output in these countries depends not only on capital inputs such as fertilizers and improved equipment, but also on improvements in technical knowledge, marketing, credit, or land tenure, for example, which are not directly reflected in the capital-output ratio.

Now the overall capital-output ratio is nothing but the average of these different sectoral capital-output ratios weighted according to the quantities of the different goods and services which are to be produced. Thus, before we can calculate the overall ratio we must specify the proportions of the different constituent items which are to make up a proposed rate of increase in the national output. But this barely scratches the surface of the problem of testing the consistency of an integrated economic development plan. For one thing, the target

1. W. B. Reddaway gives the following sectoral capital-output ratios for the third Indian five-year plan which has adopted an overall capital-output ratio of 2.2: Agriculture, 0·9; Mining and Manufacturing, 2·6; Small industries and Construction, 1·0; Railways and Communications, 6·5; Housing, 18·0; Other services, including Schools, Hospitals and Roads, 2·0. *The Development of the Indian Economy*, p. 211. It may be noted that Housing, Railways and Communications have a very high capital-output ratio. In other countries, electricity generation and supply tends to have a very high capital-output ratio (cf. S. A. Abbas, *Capital Requirements for the Development of South and Southeast Asia*, pp. 140–4). It may also be noted that, in general, manufacturing and mining industries require a relatively modest share of total investment, about a quarter of it, while the share of housing can be quite as much (cf. Colin Clark, *Conditions of Economic Progress*, third edition, pp. 604–5). The difficulties of calculating the sectoral capital-output ratios arise not only from paucity of statistical information but also from conceptual difficulties. Thus the high capital-output ratios in transport and communications should be counterbalanced by the economizing of capital stocks and inventories in other sectors, notably in commerce and distributive industries. Then there are doubtful borderline cases like fertilizer production which can be put either in the agricultural sector or in chemical industries.

G

figures of increase in outputs of various items are not given independently of each other. Many of them are required not only for final consumption but also as intermediate goods or inputs in the production of other items. In testing, therefore, the consistency of the target figures of items and the resources available for them, we must take into account not only the direct requirements but also the indirect requirements of capital. Further, these complex input-output relationships should be tested not only for a given year, but continuously over the whole period of the plan. This means that for each of the intervening years, say, during a five-year plan, the rates of expansion of the different sectors must be phased so that they dovetail into each other, without any sector lagging behind their concerted time-table and holding up the others. For if this happens, shortages and excess capacities will develop and this will alter the effective capital-output ratios in the sectors which have gone out of alignment with the general plan. By the time we have gone through the consistency of an integrated development plan in this way, it does not help us much further to 'sum up the whole thing' in the form of an overall capital-output ratio.[1]

Yet a great deal of importance has been attached to this ratio, and the real reason seems to be that it offers a convenient shorthand basis for making out the case for increasing economic aid to the underdeveloped countries. From our arithmetical example it will be seen that with a typical population growth of 2% per annum, assuming a conventional capital-output ratio between 2 and 3, a target rate of growth in per capita income between 2% and 3% commonly adopted on humanitarian grounds will require a saving-investment ratio of about 10% to 12% of national income. In the early 1950s, it was generally accepted that the underdeveloped countries were too poor to save more than about 5% of their national

1. W. B. Reddaway, *The Development of the Indian Economy*, Appendix C, for a further discussion of this concept.

income. Hence the need for massive injections of outside capital to fill this gap.

Since the early 1950s, many economists have been moving away from their simpler views of the 'capital shortage' of the underdeveloped countries based on calculations of aggregate capital requirements and overall capital-output ratios. There are many reasons for this.

First, there is now a greater recognition of the fact that a developing country's ability to save does not depend only on the level of its average national income but also on other factors such as the pattern of income distribution, the ability of the government to mobilize savings through taxation and the ability of the financial institutions making up the capital market to mobilize private savings. Many economists still work on the basis that the chief source of private savings in the under-developed countries is the ploughing-back of profits; that is to say, only the capitalists save and the landlords do not. But Professor Cairncross has pointed out that this may under-estimate the important role which the development of the capital market can play in mobilizing private savings and that in the British historical experience at least, a considerable pro-portion of these savings have come from the landowning classes.[1] Whatever the precise reason, it is interesting to note that the more recent writings on the underdeveloped countries tend to put their average saving ratio at 7% of their national income instead of the conventional level of 5% widely adopted a few years ago.[2] There is also a growing realization that some

1. A. K. Cairncross, *Factors in Economic Development*, pp. 125–8. It may also be pointed out that the real reason why capital accumulation comes to a stop in the Ricardian stationary state is not because landlords are less thrifty than capitalists, but because with a zero rate of return on capital, no one has any incentive to increase saving.

2. P. Hoffman, *One Hundred Countries and One Quarter Billion People*, and GATT *Report of International Trade 1959*; also Cairncross, op. cit., pp. 53–5.

of the developing countries may be suffering not so much from a shortage of savings in general as from the shortage in supply of particular types of goods which they need to import from abroad. This special shortage of foreign exchange as distinct from a general shortage in savings can be particularly acute for a country like India with a low ratio of export to her national income and a poor prospect of expanding her exports sufficiently to meet the rising burden of debt service payments on further borrowing.

Next, there is the remarkable fact that since the early 1950s, the idea that the rich countries should help the poor countries has become more firmly established in international opinion than earlier writers dared to hope. As Dr H. W. Singer, himself a notable champion of increasing aid to the underdeveloped countries, has pointed out: 'in the past five or six years the flow of resources to the underdeveloped countries by the medium of public aid has been a more dependable element in the flow of foreign exchange and resources to the underdeveloped countries than either export earnings, service payments, flow of private capital or any other balance of payments item. Foreign aid has steadily and year by year increased at a rate of 15% per annum from $2 billion around 1954 to around $3½ billion now (1960) without a single setback in any year.'[1] Dr Singer feels that it is time to advance beyond the simpler generalizations about 'capital shortage' which have served their purpose in rousing public opinion in favour of international aid. Many

[1]. H. W. Singer, *Recent Trends in Economic Thought on Underdeveloped Countries* (mimeographed November 1960), p. 31. Dr Singer's figures are based on the United Nations' definition of 'economic aid' which excludes short-term loans and private investment, but includes long-term loans on commercial terms from international bodies such as the World Bank and from national governments. Adopting a broader definition, Mr A. Shonfield puts the total public and private aid to the underdeveloped countries in 1958 at a figure of $5½ billion; *The Attack on World Poverty*, Appendix I. Cf. F. Benham, *Economic Aid to the Underdeveloped Countries*, Ch 2, for a good discussion of the problems of defining 'economic aid'.

economists will now share this feeling—a feeling which is strengthened by experiences in some underdeveloped countries where a considerable proportion of aid has been wasted owing to defects in organization and lack of capacity to absorb capital. Thus there has been a considerable shift in emphasis from injecting a massive dose of investment in the form of material capital, to investment in 'human capital'. Education is now increasingly regarded as the 'missing component' of economic development.

Finally, at the theoretical level, many economists are now concerned not merely with making pro-rata calculations of capital requirements on the basis of given capital-output ratios but with the further problem of whether these ratios themselves represent the most economical way of using capital in relation to the other factors of production in the underdeveloped countries.

7

The Critical Minimum Effort for Economic Development and the Size of the Balanced Growth Programme

So far I have been concerned with the case for a large-scale development effort which is based either on the historical analogy with the developed countries during their 'take-off' period, or on a desired target rate of growth in per capita income determined by political and humanitarian considerations. I shall now consider further arguments for development programmes, which are based not on value judgements but on purely general theoretical considerations about the mechanics of economic development. These arguments spring from the general thesis that the underdeveloped countries are held down very firmly to their present low levels of per capita income by 'interlocking vicious circles' which would defeat any piecemeal attempt to introduce economic development by successive steps; only a massive all-or-nothing development programme, simultaneously pushing ahead over a wide front, could hope to break the vicious circles.

I shall consider two main types of the all-or-nothing approach. The first confines itself to the overall relation between the rate of growth in per capita income and the rate of growth in population, and emphasizes that while a small increase in per capita income would be swallowed by the population increase induced by it, a large increase in per capita income created by a development programme exceeding a certain 'critical minimum effort' would enable the economy to escape the gravitational pull of population increase. The second type of approach goes beyond the overall relationships, and emphasizes the different elements of the vicious circle, particularly the low purchasing power and smallness of the market in the underdeveloped countries and the indivisibilities and interdependence of capital investment required for economic development. Thus, in order to overcome the limitations of the market created by low per capita incomes and to enjoy the internal economies of scale and external economies of complementary investment, it is necessary to start with a large-scale development programme, simultaneously trying to push forward over a wide range of economic activities. This type of approach has been developed by many writers under the general label of the 'balanced growth' theory.

The low-level equilibrium trap and the critical minimum effort thesis[1]

Essentially, this theory is based on two propositions. (i) The first proposition starts from the Malthusian theorem that population will increase when the per capita income of a country rises above the 'minimum subsistence level'. But it then goes on to state that while initially population grows rapidly with a rise in per capita income, there is an upper physical limit to the rate of population growth, say at about 3% per annum. Beyond this limit a rise in per capita income will not be accompanied by a further rise in the rate of growth of population. On the contrary, the rate of population growth may even decline gradually with further rises in per capita income; this is sug-

---

1. R. R. Nelson, 'A Theory of the Low Level Equilibrium Trap', *American Economic Review*, December 1956; and H. Leibenstein, *A Theory of Economic-Demographic Development*, and *Economic Backwardness and Economic Growth*.

gested by the experience of the Western countries, and more recently by Japan.

(ii) The second proposition consists of the familiar argument that at low levels of per capita income people are too poor to save and invest much, and this low rate of investment will result in a low rate of growth in total national income. But as the per capita income rises above a certain minimum level at which there is zero saving a rising proportion of the total income will be saved and invested and this will lead to a higher rate of growth in income.

The argument may be illustrated by a set of diagrams. In diagram (a), the level of per capita income is measured on the horizontal axis and the percentage rate of growth of population on the vertical axis. The point S on the horizontal axis denotes the minimum subsistence level of per capita income. Below this level of income to the left of S, population will be decreasing, and at S population will be stationary. But as we move to the right of S, denoting a rise in the per capita income above the subsistence level, the rate of population growth depicted by the PP' curve will increase until it reaches the upper physical limit around 3% after which it may decline gradually. In diagram (b) the level of per capita income is measured on the horizontal axis as before, but the vertical axis measures the per capita rate of investment out of savings at different levels of per capita income. The point X on the horizontal axis denotes the level of income with zero saving. Until this level of income is reached, all income will be spent on consumption, and below this level, to the left of X, there is negative investment, or living on past capital. But as we move to the right of X, denoting a rise in the per capita income above the zero saving level, the per capita rate of investment, the II' curve, will rise and there is no upper limit to it. As we move to the right of X, a rising proportion of the total income can be saved and invested, particularly beyond the point at which the rate of growth in population

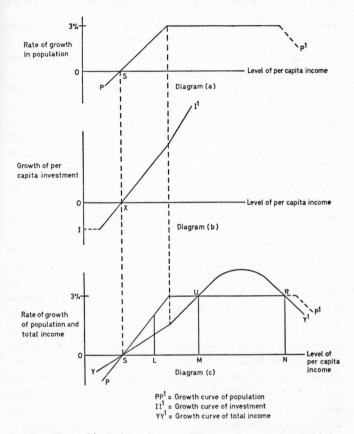

Rate of growth
in population

3%

O — Level of per capita income

P' S

Diagram (a)

Growth of per
capita investment

I¹

O — Level of per capita income

X

I

Diagram (b)

Rate of growth
of population and
total income

3%

U

R

P¹

Y¹

O — Level of
per capita
income

Y

S L M N

P

Diagram (c)

PP¹ = Growth curve of population
II¹ = Growth curve of investment
YY¹ = Growth curve of total income

levels off at 3%. It is only at a later stage at a much higher income level that the proportion of total income saved and invested will settle down to a constant fraction.

There is no necessity for the minimum subsistence level of per capita income S to be the same as the zero saving level of per capita income X. But for simplicity's sake, I have drawn the diagram (c) on the assumption that the two coincide. Here, as before, the horizontal axis measures the level of per capita income. But on the vertical axis we are now measuring the percentage rate of growth in population and the percentage rate of growth in total income at the different levels of per capita income shown along the horizontal axis. As I have drawn the diagram, the point S (equal to X) on the horizontal axis represents the 'low-level equilibrium' trap. It denotes the intersection of the population growth curve PP′ and the income growth curve YY′ at the zero rate of growth. Starting from this, for any small rise in the level of per capita income, say of SL, the rate of growth in population will be higher than the rate of growth in total income, pushing back the per capita income to its previous stable equilibrium level of OS. This low-level equilibrium trap will be stronger the more quickly the rate of population growth responds to a given rise in per capita income and the more slowly the rate of growth in total income responds to an increase in investment, due, say, to initial population pressure on land. But if it were possible to raise the level of per capita income by a discontinuous jump by more than SM, which means pushing the rate of increase in income beyond the population barrier of 3%, then we should have arrived at a new unstable equilibrium at U. A rise in the level of per capita income beyond OM, being unaccompanied by a further rise in the rate of population growth, would then lead to a cumulative process of rising income until possibly it reached a new stable equilibrium point R with a per capita income level of ON.

The 'critical minimum effort' theory has given us a very neat formalization of the vicious circle of low per capita income, leading to low rate of saving and investment, leading to a low per capita income. But it raises two sets of difficulties.

First, we may question whether it is possible to draw a rigid functional relation between the level of per capita income and the rate of growth of population and the rate of growth in total income. As we have seen in Chapter 2, the main cause of growth in population has been the reduction in death rates due to improvements in public health and the control of epidemics and endemics, which are not closely related to a prior rise in per capita income level. The tendency of a rise in per capita income to *lower* birth rates at higher income levels needs to be interpreted even more cautiously. But we may on the whole accept the upper physical limit to the rate of population growth around 3% per annum, provided it is clearly understood that even beyond this point the absolute size of population would continue to grow at a constant or slowly diminishing rate, continuing to exert its pressure on the given natural resources. The functional relationship between the level of per capita income and the rate of growth in total income is more complex and takes place in two steps. The relation between the level of per capita income and the rate of saving and investment is modified by a number of factors such as the pattern of distribution of incomes and the effectiveness of financial institutions in mobilizing savings. The relation between investment and the resultant output is also not given by a stable overall capital-output ratio, but depends on how far the productive organization of the country can be improved and how far land-saving innovations can be adopted to overcome the tendency to diminishing returns on additional investment which will continue even after the population growth has levelled off at 3% per annum.

The second set of difficulties arises from the complications introduced by the 'time element'. It may be noted that the diagrams illustrate a set of 'timeless' functional relationships rather than the time-series of growth in population and income. Further, the analytical device of using two reaction curves which intersect first at a 'stable' and then at an 'unstable' equilibrium as in diagram (c) is borrowed from the Trade Cycle theory designed to deal with turning points in the level of short-run economic activity in the advanced countries—from a state of depression through an 'upswing' phase to a

boom and so on.[1] We may therefore question how far this type
of analysis, originally designed to illustrate the gear-shifts in
short-run economic activity of a fully developed engine of
growth in the advanced countries, is useful for the study of the
problem of the long-term economic development of the underdeveloped countries which is concerned with the construction
of the engine of growth itself.

Two specific points may be raised. Consider first a 'small'
rise in the level of per capita income from S to an intermediate
point L below OM in diagram (c). This will lead back to the
'stable' equilibrium point S only if we interpret the curves as
timeless and reversible relations. If we take the time factor into
account, the rise of income from S to L may be accompanied
by permanent and 'irreversible' additions to the capital stock
and skills. In this case, things will not be exactly the same as
before and the economy may not revert to the previous level of
per capita income S but may stay at a point above it. Once we
admit the possibility of the 'ratchet effect',[2] the case for a large
'critical minimum effort' to reach OM at one go is considerably
weakened since we may be able to get there by a series of smaller
steps supported by a ratchet at each step. Next, consider that
by a massive development programme a country has succeeded
for a time in raising the rate of growth in its total income above
the 3% per annum rate which represents the population barrier.
Does this really mean that at the per capita level above OM it
has now automatically entered a new 'unstable' phase of cumulative upward rise in income? Clearly this is not so since it is
not difficult to find examples of abortive 'take-offs' in which a
country may for a time succeed in raising its saving and investment ratio above 10% to 12% and raising the rate of growth
in its total income above the 3% level, but subsequently

1. e.g. N. Kaldor, 'A Model of the Trade Cycle', *Economic Journal*,
March 1940.
2. I owe this point to Mr A. D. Knox.

relapse into a slower rate of growth and stagnation. How long must a country sustain its rate of growth above the 3% level before it can be sure of breaking through the population barrier? Whatever its drawbacks, the 'take-off' theory at least suggests by means of historical examples that this effort has to be sustained for two or three decades during which fundamental reorganizations in the institutional and productive structure should be taking place. On the other hand, the neat geometrical model of the 'critical minimum effort' theory is not designed to deal with these longer-term problems of changes in the economic and social framework which ensure a successful 'take-off'.

The size of the balanced growth

Balanced growth theory may refer to the minimum *size* of the investment programme required to start economic development. Or it may refer to the *path* of economic development and the pattern of investment necessary to keep the different sectors of the economy in a balanced growth relation with each other. I shall start with the first aspect of the theory which stresses the need for an all-or-nothing approach to economic development. It is possible to distinguish at least three related versions of the theory, each suggesting a progressively larger aggregate size of the balanced growth investment programme than its predecessor.

(a) The earliest and the narrowest version of the theory is to be found in Professor P. N. Rosenstein-Rodan's well-known article first published in 1943.[1] The central idea here is the need to overcome the smallness in the size of the market created by the low per capita income and purchasing power of consumers in the underdeveloped countries. He argues that a single

1. P. N. Rosenstein-Rodan, 'Problems of Industrialization of Eastern and South-Eastern Europe', *Economic Journal*, 1943.

factory, even when it uses more efficient methods of production than the handicraft industry, may fail when set up on its own because of the smallness of the market outlet for its output. What is needed is the simultaneous setting up of a number of factories producing different consumers' goods so that between them they create enough new employment and purchasing power to provide a sufficiently large market for each other. This is the narrowest version of the theory in that it confines the balanced growth programme to the production of light consumers' goods. It was assumed that Eastern and South-Eastern Europe as a region would be exporting agricultural products and importing machinery and equipment from abroad so that heavy industry and agriculture were explicitly excluded from the framework of the programme. It was also assumed that the region as a whole was adequately supplied with transport, communications and power for the setting up of consumers' goods industries so that there was no need for costly investment in social overhead capital to support the programme. Considering the abundant supply of 'disguised unemployment' from agriculture, all that was needed was a sufficient inflow of outside capital to finance a sufficiently large balanced-growth programme in consumers' goods with markets for them from the whole region. The argument was that starting from the low levels of income and consumption of the people of the region, it would not be difficult to predict the extra amounts of different consumers' goods which they would demand with a rise in their incomes. It was also pointed out that by concentrating on the production of consumers' goods the balanced growth approach would provide a less painful alternative to the 'communist model' of industrialization with its emphasis on setting up heavy capital goods industries at the expense of consumers' goods.

To get at the logical basis of the argument, let us start from the initial situation where the consumers' goods to be included in the balanced growth programme were either produced by the handicraft industries or were imported at *a certain set of relative prices*. Starting from this, it is possible to think of two extreme cases showing the relative importance of pure cost reduction and pure income expansion for the success of the new industries.

First, let us suppose the rise of an especially capable entre-preneur or an improvement in the techniques of production in one of the consumers' goods industries. In this case, it is clearly possible for a single new factory producing this par-ticular product to establish itself successfully, in spite of the prevailing low incomes and purchasing power of its customers. The total size of the market may be limited; but if the new factory is efficient enough, it can attract a share of this total market sufficient to enable it to use its machinery and fixed equipment to full capacity and reduce the cost per unit of its output to a minimum. By lowering its price, the new factory is able to attract customers, not only from the handicraft industry which was producing a similar product, but also from all other consumers' goods whose prices have remained the same as before. Through sheer efficiency and ability to reduce cost, a single new factory can establish itself successfully, relying mainly on the 'substitution effect' working through the price elasticity of demand for its product. In displacing the demand for some of the existing products, the new factory will cause some unemployment elsewhere; but, provided it can create enough new employment to offset this, the total income and purchasing power will be increased, since the resources em-ployed in the new factory now have higher productivity. But this favourable 'income effect' is likely to be of secondary importance to the success of the new factory.

Next, at the other extreme, let us think of setting up a large group of new factories producing different consumers' goods whose individual productive efficiency is not superior to that of the existing producers of these goods. These new factories would then have to rely on their combined ability to expand employment and purchasing power to be able to sell their products at the same prices as before. It will be seen that by relying mainly on the 'income effect', and without the ability to reduce costs and so attract the extra demand from outside the group, the new factories as a group are not likely to create enough extra purchasing power to be able to dispose of their combined output. First, since the value of the total output of the new factories is made up of wages and profit, expenditure out of the new wage income alone could not create a sufficient extra demand. This gap in purchasing power has to be filled by assuming that all the profits are re-invested and turned into wage-income elsewhere, say in the capital goods industries whose workers now become the customers for the newly produced consumers' goods. Further, in so far as the balanced growth programme embraces only a part of the economy, there would be leakages of purchasing power to other sectors outside its framework; say in the form of extra demand for food from the agricultural sector, the extra demand for the products of the handicraft and other indigenous industries, and the extra demand for imports.

The situation depicted in this version (a) of the balanced growth theory seems to lie between these two cases of pure cost reduction and pure income expansion, but with considerable leanings towards pure income expansion. It does not assume any special improvements in the methods of production or the rise of a superior entrepreneurial class, for these would dispense with the need for a balanced growth programme. On the other hand, it does assume that merely by taking over the existing technical 'know-how' of the advanced countries, the new factories would normally be able to reduce their costs below the handicraft industries, provided that each could obtain individual markets large enough to expand output to full capacity production, reducing its cost per unit to a minimum.

I now come to the crucial link in the argument. By insisting that a large number of factories should be set up at the same time, the theory concentrates on the enlargement of the total volume of purchasing power and the *total size* of the market. On the other hand, the ability of each factory to obtain the economies of the modern factory method of production depends on its share of the total market: that is, on the size of its *individual* market. The theory then assumes too readily that, provided the size of the total market can be increased, the share of the individual market accruing to each factory will follow a set pattern of expansion in consumers' expenditure, determined by the income elasticity of demand for each product. Thus provided that the total volume of employment and purchasing power is increased by a 'minimum' indivisible step, each factory will have a large enough market to reach full capacity production and the point of minimum cost per unit. There are three weaknesses in this argument.

First, the introduction of the existing technical 'know-how' of the advanced countries to the different conditions that exist in the underdeveloped countries need not always result in the superiority of the modern factory method of production over the existing indigenous methods. It largely depends on how well these modern techniques are adapted to local conditions; that is, on the skill and quality of the entrepreneurs who run new factories. Again, in any given condition, the 'normal' superiority of factory methods over handicraft methods will vary widely between different commodities: given a large group of new factories, the capacity of each individual factory to reduce its cost below existing producers will vary very widely. At one end of the scale there would be 'stronger' factories which could almost stand up on their own, and at the other end of the scale there would be 'weaker' factories whose costs, even

H

at full capacity production, would be barely below those of the handicraft industries. These weaker factories are the 'marginal' factories whose inclusion into the programme would have to be carefully examined. Secondly, for the type of light consumers' goods with which the version (a) of the theory is concerned, the 'substitution effect' and price elasticities of demand are likely to play a much larger role than the theory allows. Finally, there is no reason to suppose that the pattern of expansion of consumers' expenditure on different goods, determined by their respective income elasticities of demand, would fit in neatly with the pattern of expansion in the supplies of these goods, representing full-capacity production or the technically indivisible quantum of expansion for each. These disproportions can only be corrected through changes in relative prices.

Once we recognize the importance of the 'substitution effect' working through the changes in relative costs and prices and price elasticities of demand, the all-or-none approach to economic development formulated entirely in terms of the 'income effect' and income elasticities of demand becomes illusory. The whole argument seems to be incomplete and indeterminate if it does not take into account changes in the relative costs and prices. The success of the balanced growth programme of type (a) depends not merely on how many factories are being set up at the same time, but more importantly on the varying degrees of superior efficiency each factory has over the existing producers, and on each factory's ability to counter the potential leakage of purchasing power outside by reductions in costs and prices.

But can we not go on expanding the size of the balanced growth programme by setting up more factories until the sheer size of the 'income effect' overcomes the weakness of the 'substitution effect' in favour of the programme? It is worth emphasizing that even on the assumptions (i) that an 'unlimited' supply of labour would be available from 'disguised unemployment' and (ii) that a sufficient amount of external capital would be forthcoming to pay for the machinery and capital equipment to be used for the production of consumers' goods, a continued expansion in the size of the programme is likely to be subject to sharply increasing costs for at least three reasons. First, as we have seen, the increasing volume of employment in the new factories would be likely to increase the pressure of demand for food and, in so far as agriculture is subject to diminishing returns, this would raise the cost of living and the money wage costs in the manufacturing sector in the Ricardian manner. Secondly, even if a large number of factories were to create economies in the training and 'skilling' of labour in the longer run, the immediate effect would be for each factory to bid up the wages of the scarce skilled labour and create external diseconomies for each other. Finally, there is likely to be a serious shortage of suitable entrepreneurs and managers for the factories, and as less able people were recruited to these positions there would be a general decline in efficiency and increasing costs. Thus, the possible favourable income effect of increasing the size of the programme has to be weighed against the possible sharp rise in costs as an increasing number of factories compete for scarce resources in the form of food supply, skilled labour and entrepreneurs and managers. Instead of an all-or-none approach, we are led back to the more familiar procedure of making economic choices between a smaller and a larger size of development plan, even if this is a more rough-and-ready process than the traditional marginal calculus in terms of very small incremental gains and losses.

(b) As soon as the first version of the balanced growth theory is applied to the underdeveloped countries of Asia and Africa with their inadequate transport and communication and power supply, its exponents feel the need to extend its framework to include investment in these 'social overhead' services. Now investment of this type is notoriously 'lumpy' in the sense that a power station or a transport system has to be fairly large to be able to provide its services at economically feasible costs. Thus, we have the second version of the balanced growth theory: this emphasizes the 'technical indivisibilities' in social overhead capital and the need to have a balance between the public utilities providing transport, communications and power on the one hand, and the factories producing consumers' goods on the other, avoiding bottlenecks and excess capacities in the public utilities. In addition to their 'lumpiness', the capital-output ratio in the social overhead services is higher than in most other industries. The aggregate capital requirements of the balanced growth programme of type (b), therefore, are much larger than those of type (a).

Technical indivisibilities in social overhead capital are undoubtedly very important. But even here it is necessary to point out two serious qualifications to the argument that an underdeveloped country cannot start developing unless it is provided beforehand with a complete outfit of transport and communications, power supply and other social overhead services. First, even in Asia and Africa, different underdeveloped countries already possess these social overhead facilities in varying degrees, depending on their history and geography. For most of these countries, the practical question is not whether to have a completely new outfit of these services starting from scratch, but how much to extend and improve the existing facilities. For instance, the typical choices involved are whether to extend the main railway line or have more feeder lines; whether to extend the road services instead of the railway services; whether to improve existing roads between towns or open up the remoter parts of the country; whether to have smaller power stations combined with wells for irrigation instead of a giant multi-purpose river valley project; and many more. Secondly, even if it is accepted that in the particular circumstances of a country a certain fairly large 'indivisible' social overhead investment is necessary, the fact remains that such a large project cannot be immediately completed to support a simultaneous expansion of consumers' goods industries. A project like this inevitably takes time to construct, and furthermore it is generally capable of being phased for completion over a longer or a shorter period. This possibility of changing the phasing and the time dimension of the project therefore introduces a considerable flexibility to the economic (as distinct from the technical) size of an 'indivisible' social overhead investment. In deciding how quickly a particular large-scale social overhead project should be completed, we should have to compare the costs and inconveniences of putting up with the existing bottlenecks for a time with the extra costs and diseconomies of hurrying up its completion. It may be noted that accelerating the rate of completion of a particular investment project is subject to increasing costs in the same way as increasing the size of a programme for a given period. We may therefore conclude that although the technical indivisibilities in social overhead capital are undoubtedly very important, they are not sufficient to bear the weight of the all-or-nothing approach to economic development suggested by the version (b) of the balanced growth theory.

(c) The third version of the balanced growth theory, the 'big push',[1] is nothing short of an attempt to introduce a comprehensive and integrated programme of industrialization, including within its framework not only the consumers' goods industries and social overhead investment but also capital goods industries. The only thing left out here seems to be the agricultural sector. It is argued that in order to launch economic development successfully, it is necessary not only to enlarge the size of the market and obtain the 'internal economies' of

1. P. N. Rosenstein-Rodan, 'Notes on the Theory of the "Big Push" ', *Economic Development for Latin America*, ed. H. S. Ellis, London, Macmillan, 1951.

large-scale production, but also to obtain the 'external economies' which arise from simultaneously setting up industries which are technically interdependent with each other; that while these 'technical complementarities' do not normally exist between a horizontal group of consumers' goods industries at the same stage of production, they are very important between a vertical group of industries at different stages of production; and that since these external economies are particularly important in the capital goods industries which supply each other and the consumers' goods industries with various inputs in the form of machinery and semi-processed intermediate goods, the capital goods sector should form an integral part of the balanced growth programme. This comprehensive version of the theory therefore tries to fulfil simultaneously three sets of balanced growth relations: (i) the horizontal balance between different consumers' goods industries determined by the pattern of expansion in consumers' demand; (ii) the balance between social overhead investment and the directly productive activities both in the consumers' and the capital goods sectors; and (iii) the vertical balance between the capital goods industries, including the intermediate goods and the consumers' goods industries, determined by the technical complementarities.

Two main features stand out in this version (c) of the theory. The first is the 'external economies' argument: in pursuing this we shall be led to some of the issues involved in the question of the relative importance of planning and free enterprise in promoting economic development in the underdeveloped countries. The second is the argument for comprehensive programming which has been likened to an attempt to impose a complete and brand new 'second floor' on the weak and imperfectly developed one-floor economy of these countries. In examining this argument for comprehensiveness, we shall see the basic weakness of the all-or-nothing approach which is more pronounced in version (c) than in the previous versions.

In welfare economics, 'external economies' are defined as unpaid services which accrue to third parties. These are not fully reflected in private costs and products so that the market prices have to be corrected to take them into account. In the development literature, the concept is used in a different sense. The 'external economies' are the 'pecuniary' economies trans- mitted through the price system. They originate in a given industry A (say due to the internal economies of overcoming technical indivisibilities) and are then passed on in the form of a lower price for A's product to another industry B which uses it as an input or a factor of production. New investment in A which overcomes its technical indivisibilities will cheapen its product. 'The profits of industry B created by the lower price of factor A, call for investment and expansion in industry B, one result of which will be an increase in industry B's demand for industry A's product. This in its turn will give rise to profits and call for further investment and expansion of industry A'.[1]

Now it is argued that this mutually beneficial type of expan- sion in output will not take place to the fullest possible extent without a balanced growth planning. This is so, first, because of the inadequacy of free market prices to act as a signalling device informing private investors about *future* possibilities of expansion in the complementary industries A and B; and secondly because of the imperfect response of private enterprise in the underdeveloped countries to a given signal from the price system. In order to reap the 'external economies' to the full extent, the investment in the two complementary industries would have to be planned together and carried out in an inte- grated way by a planning authority.

It is true that with an embryonic or imperfectly developed capital market and 'futures' market, the price mechanism in most underdeveloped countries is a very poor signalling system,

1. T. Scitovsky, 'Two Concepts of External Economies', *Journal of Political Economy*, April 1954.

particularly about future events. But on the other hand, the institutional and administrative machinery available for the governments of the underdeveloped countries is also, with a few exceptions, notoriously weak. It is difficult, therefore, to generalize whether the communication system about future events will always improve with a greater degree of state planning, without taking into account the particular circumstances of each case.

The general problems of co-ordinating a complex integrated development plan of the type required by version (c) of the balanced growth theory are well known, and they are frequently thought to be beyond the competence even of the stronger and more efficient governmental machinery of the advanced countries. Two points may however be emphasized. First, the governments of the underdeveloped countries are likely to face their greatest difficulties, not in the initial drawing up of the economic development plans (frequently done with the assistance of foreign experts), but in the execution of the various projects according to a planned time-table and in keeping the different departments and agencies *continually informed* about progress in carrying out the plans. In carrying out a complex set of related projects, there are bound to be various revisions of the original plans, delays and departures from the original time-table. The greater the interdependence between the different components of the plan, the greater the repercussions of an unexpected or unavoidable change in one part of the plan on the rest, and the greater the need to keep the different parts of the plans continually revised in the light of the latest available information. These problems of co-ordination, even within the different parts of the public sector, are formidable, and it is not surprising if 'progress reporting' remains one of the weakest parts of the planning machinery. Secondly, one of the most serious gaps in knowledge required for planning is likely to arise, not merely from a lack of general 'technical know-how' but from ignorance of the local conditions in the underdeveloped countries themselves, and inefficient 'feed-back' of this vital local knowledge from the different parts of the country to the central planning machinery. Nor can this be easily remedied, as is commonly supposed, by improving the standard type of statistical information. Frequently local information relevant for efficient planning depends on the qualitative differences and local peculiarities which are ab-stracted from the statistical compilations concerned with ob-taining comparable sets of figures for the country as a whole.

So far we have been concerned with the problems of co-ordination between the different parts of the government sector. But most underdeveloped countries have a consider-able private sector in agriculture and consumers' goods indus-tries, traditional and modern; and some countries like India have an important private sector even in the capital goods industries. Thus, in order to assess a comprehensive balanced growth programme, we have to take into account the rather neglected problem of economic development in the 'mixed economy', viz. the problem of co-ordination between the government and the private sector. The problem is simpler when the two sectors are complementary; for instance, the govern-ment may inform the private sector about its future plans to expand transport and communications or power and may expect the private sector to embark on complementary investment (even here uncertainties about time-tables for the completion of government projects can create difficulties). The problem of co-ordination and communication becomes formidable when the two sectors are competitive, say either because the govern-ment is planning to set up factories to compete with private firms in a given industry or threatening to nationalize private competitors, or because both the government and the private sector are competing for some scarce resources, normally the limited foreign exchange reserves of the country. In this situa-tion, a 'cold war' has developed between the two sectors in many underdeveloped countries. The government departments tend to keep their plans and intentions secret from the private businessmen because they fear 'speculative' activities which will disrupt their plans. On the other hand, private enterprise is inhibited by uncertainties not only about the general economic situation but also about the future intentions of the government and future changes in government regulations. These uncertainties are aggravated when the government, with its drive for a large-scale development plan straining its resources, gets itself into a 'crisis' situation where it is obliged to resort to sudden tightening of controls, notably foreign exchange controls, which upset not only its own plans but also those of the private sector.

Thus, it seems too optimistic to hope that the adoption of comprehensive balanced-growth investment planning by itself, without fundamental improvements in the administrative machinery of the government, and the easing of mutual distrust and suspicion between the government and the private sectors, would improve the efficiency of signalling and co-ordination between the different sectors of the economy.

Let us now pass on to the question of the responsiveness of private enterprise in underdeveloped countries to a given signal from the price system. Logically, the fact that two industries A and B are complementary does not necessarily mean that they should be expanded simultaneously to reach the maximum possible expansion for both. With the responsiveness of private enterprise, this expansion may be achieved either by expanding A to the full extent and inducing B to expand correspondingly by lowering the price of the input A, or by expanding B to the full extent, inducing A to expand correspondingly under the pressure of excess demand for its product by B. In the advanced countries, this may take place through private initiative only, resulting in what is known as 'vertical integration'. Even in the underdeveloped countries, the state may need to expand through its own initiative either A or B only, rather than both as suggested by the balanced growth theory.

Stressing this possibility, Professor Hirschman has built up an alternative strategy of economic development: the deliberately 'unbalanced growth' approach.[1] He agrees with the balanced growth theorists about the importance of technical complementarities between industries at different stages of production which he calls 'vertical linkages', but arrives at the opposite conclusion by introducing two further propositions.

First, he points out that the degree of complementarity is stronger between some particular groups of industries than others. Thus the aim of development policy should be not to push forward simultaneously on all fronts as though these complementarities were uniformly distributed all over the economy, but to select and concentrate on particular 'strategic' sectors of the economy where these interdependent linkage effects may be expected to be strongest. He believes that these strategic parts of the economy are to be found where the network of input-output relationships is thickest, representing industries which buy the largest part of their inputs from other industries, or sell the largest part of their outputs to other industries (as distinct from the final consumers), or both.

Secondly, he argues that the balanced growth approach, even if it were successful, will merely achieve a once-for-all increase in national income, coming to rest at a higher plateau representing the balanced growth equilibrium. Economic development, however, should be a continuous dynamic process, kept alive by the tensions of shortages and excess supplies and by the disequilibria in the strategic sectors which are capable of responding to these pace-setting pressures. The balanced growth theorists would like the two complementary industries A and B to expand simultaneously to their 'full' equilibrium

1. A. O. Hirschman, *The Strategy of Economic Development*, Chs. 3-6.

level which would exhaust the external economies possible in the initial situation. Professor Hirschman would like either A or B to overshoot the equilibrium point. He hopes that the resulting pressures of excess demand or excess supply would change the initial situation itself and lead to further economic development in a series of 'leap-frogging' movements.

The whole question depends to a large extent on the assumption we make about the responsiveness of private enterprise in the underdeveloped countries to a disequilibrium situation with profitable opportunities of increasing investment. The balanced growth theorists are thinking of a situation where the complementary industries are new industries requiring a considerable initial outlay of capital and technical experience on the part of the new entrants into them. They feel that it is beyond the capacity of unaided private enterprise in the underdeveloped countries to respond effectively to this situation so that the government must take the initiative in launching a balanced growth programme. There are, however, considerable differences among the balanced growth theorists themselves over the question how much of the programme should be directly carried by the government planning authority. Some are content merely to point out the theoretical advantages of the balanced growth approach without specifying the exact proportion of the 'mixed economy'. Others are contemptuous about 'patching up the market' and imply that the bulk of the balanced growth programme, not only in the social overhead capital but also in the capital and the consumers' goods sectors, should be carried out by state enterprise.

The popular argument concerning the shortage of entrepreneurs in the underdeveloped countries, however, is not a sufficient reason for increasing the government sector. For if the private sector suffers from a shortage of entrepreneurs, the government sector will equally suffer from a shortage of administrators who can perform these entrepreneurial functions. As

Professor Hirschman has pointed out, the balanced growth approach makes an impossible demand on the underdeveloped countries by requiring them to provide, all at once, entrepreneurs and managers to run a whole flock of new industries; if they could do this, they would not be underdeveloped in the first place. But he believes that the problem of increasing the supply of entrepreneurs and capital can be solved in the long run, provided the right type of pressures are used to bring them forth. He believes that, if suitable investment opportunities are opened up by his unbalanced growth approach, additional supplies of domestic savings will be forthcoming, and that what is holding back many underdeveloped countries is not so much the shortage of savings as the 'ability to invest'. Similarly, the unbalanced growth approach may be regarded as providing a school for entrepreneurs, spelling out their profit opportunities in block letters by means of deliberately engineered bottlenecks and excess capacities, and thus assisting the 'learning process' of the potential entrepreneurs in the underdeveloped countries.

Other aspects of the controversy between the balanced growth and the unbalanced growth approaches will be considered in Chapters 9 and 10. For the moment, I shall conclude this chapter by pointing out the basic weakness of the all-or-nothing approach which version (c) of the balanced growth theory suffers from more than the previous versions. The crucial practical question which faces the developing countries is not how to plan their development programmes as though they had unlimited supplies of resources, but what sort of choices they should make when their currently available resources are insufficient for a comprehensive balanced growth programme. The question of having to make unpalatable choices has been pushed into the background, first by the assumption of the 'unlimited supply of labour' and second by the expectation of greater foreign aid. In the previous chapter, we have already seen that the cushion provided by the economic potential from 'disguised unemployment' is very thin. So now the main reliance has to be placed on greater foreign aid. But however generous the supply of foreign aid, it can only relieve the harshness of choices rather than abolish the basic economic problem of having to make choices. This is particularly true when it is remembered that in many underdeveloped countries the basic 'scarce factor' may not be the shortage of saving but the ability to absorb and invest capital effectively. It is the basic weakness of the various versions of the balanced growth theories that they obscure this problem of choice. The more comprehensive the minimum size of the development programme they advocate, the more the problem of choice is obscured.

For instance, the version (a) obscures the choices within the consumers' goods sector, but at an overall level the choice it makes is clear. If the underdeveloped countries do not have enough resources to push ahead on all fronts, they should concentrate on investment in consumers' goods industries, assuming the necessary capital goods can be imported through trade or aid. This choice is made on the basis that the limitation in the size of the market is the most important obstacle to economic development, and that the existing levels of consumption are so low that it is better to try to raise consumption immediately even at the cost of a slower rate of economic growth in the future. The converse of version (a), the 'communist model' of industrialization, also makes a clear-cut choice, in favour of the capital goods sector. This is done presumably on the basis that the most important requirement for economic development is to be able to reap the technical economies of scale and complementarities, and that since these are most abundant in the capital goods sector, it is better to sacrifice present consumption for the sake of the faster rate of future economic growth. The 'big push' or the version (c) of the balanced growth theory, however, insists on expanding investment, not only in the consumers' goods industries, but in the capital goods industries and also in the public utilities and social overhead capital. By insisting on this simultaneous expansion on all fronts, it has not only evaded the crucial economic choices between present and future income, but has frequently encouraged many underdeveloped countries to push too far beyond their currently available resources and organizing ability. This is frequently defended on the grounds that it might elicit more foreign aid. It is questionable, however, whether the prospect of foreign aid, which is far from certain, is sufficient to justify pushing the developing countries into a 'crisis' situation in which they are no longer in a position to make any coherent or consistent choices and are merely driven from one ad hoc emergency measure to another. This is surely the reverse of 'economic planning'.

8

The Path of Balanced Growth and the Rate of Economic Development

Let us now turn from the *size* to the *path* of balanced growth. Instead of the minimum size of the balanced growth programme required to start economic development successfully, I am now concerned with the rate of economic development which can be sustained over a period of time, by expanding the output of the different sectors of the economy in a balanced growth relation. The exponents of the balanced growth path theory, notably Professors Lewis and Nurkse,[1] explicitly regard agriculture also as one of the 'industries' to be included in the balanced growth framework. Thus, while the previous versions of the theory were mainly concerned with the balanced growth within the manufacturing sector only, emphasis has now shifted to the broad inter-sectoral balance between agriculture and manufactures, each sector providing the market and supplying the necessary ingredients for the expansion of the other. The balanced growth path theory, therefore, may be looked upon as two-edged criticism, both of the orthodox view that the underdeveloped countries should specialize in primary export production for which they have a comparative advantage, and of the modern view that they should embark on an all-out drive for industrialization.

1. W. A. Lewis, *Theory of Economic Growth*, pp. 276–83; R. Nurkse, *The Conflict Between 'Balanced Growth' and International Specialization*, Istanbul and Ankara, and *Patterns of Trade and Development*, Wicksell Lectures, 1959.

The possible conflict between international specialization and internal balanced growth, particularly for those underdeveloped countries not suffering from overpopulation, will be discussed in the next chapter. For the moment, I shall concentrate on the internal and domestic aspects of the balanced growth path in relation to industrialization and the rate of economic development, and in the setting of the overpopulated underdeveloped countries.

Industrialization is popularly regarded as synonymous with economic development by the people of the developing countries. They feel that agriculture is an inherently less productive occupation than manufacturing industry,[1] and that the present economic structure of their countries, characterized by a large proportion of the total working force in primary production, is somehow lop-sided and unbalanced and should be cured by an all-out drive for manufacturing industry. It is not unfair to say that this bias in favour of industrialization seems to be shared even by the economists who advocate the 'balanced growth' approach of the type we have examined in the last chapter, with its emphasis on balanced growth only within the manufacturing sector. This bias for manufacturing industry seems to arise partly out of a desire to find something which can absorb the rural surplus labour and partly out of the feeling that, before the developing countries can proceed along the balanced growth path, their initial imbalance between agriculture and

1. This belief may also derive from statistical correlations showing that while countries with high per capita incomes have a larger proportion of their labour in secondary and tertiary industries, countries with low per capita incomes have a larger proportion of their labour in primary production. What is not always clearly understood is that the higher proportion of labour in secondary and tertiary industries may be the consequence and not the cause of higher per capita incomes, reflecting the well-known tendency of people to spend more on manufactures and services and less on food as their income rises. For further discussion of this subject see P. T. Bauer and B. S. Yamey, 'Economic Progress and Occupational Distribution', *Economic Journal*, December 1951.

I

manufacturing industry must be cured by starting with a counterbalancing expansion of the manufacturing industry.

The bottleneck in agriculture

Some of the weaknesses in the argument for a one-sided drive to expand the manufacturing sector can be seen once we try to apply the balanced growth path approach systematically. To begin with, it is not possible to say that there is an 'imbalance' between agriculture and industry in an underdeveloped country simply because the larger proportion of its labour and other resources is employed in agriculture. What is relevant is not the present proportion of *resources* in the two sectors but the future rate of expansion in the *output* of the two sectors. In a closed economy, the fact that a larger proportion of its labour is employed in agriculture does mean that productivity in agriculture is low and that it requires a large number of workers in agriculture to support a non-agricultural worker in the rest of the economy. But this cannot be cured simply by trying to transfer labour from agriculture to manufacturing. Indeed, this transfer will not be possible unless the productivity of the agricultural sector is raised simultaneously, enabling it to feed a larger number of industrial workers. A reduction in the over-crowding on land may be necessary as a method of facilitating the improvement in agricultural productivity. But the essential point is that the manufacturing sector cannot continue to expand for long without a balanced expansion in the output of the agricultural sector. Given the logic of the balanced growth path, the rate of development of the whole economy will be determined by the rate of expansion in its slowest moving component part; and given the tendency to diminishing returns, agriculture clearly qualifies for this role as the major bottleneck. Thus, even if the manufacturing sector can import the durable capital goods from abroad, its rate of expansion will ultimately depend on the rate of expansion in the output of the agricultural sector.

In Chapter 6 we have seen that rural overpopulation characterized by the 'zero marginal product of labour' does not automatically ensure that the 'disguised unemployment' can be removed without reducing the total agricultural output and therefore that there would be a food surplus waiting to be mobilized to feed non-agricultural workers. With given agricultural techniques, total output will remain unchanged only on condition that the same total amount of work continues to be applied to the land. This means that those who are left behind on the land after the surplus workers are removed must somehow be induced to put in the extra work to maintain the same total volume of work as before. This question assumes a dominating importance when we are concerned not merely with maintaining a particular total agricultural output and a once-for-all transfer of the food surplus but with trying to have a continually expanding food surplus from the agricultural sector to feed the expanding labour force in the manufacturing sector.

There are two main approaches to the problem of expanding the output of the agricultural sector. On the one hand, there are positive economic incentives to induce the farmers to expand their marketable surplus. This requires that an expanding stream of manufactured consumers' goods should be available, on attractive terms, for exchange with the agricultural produce. Thus, the crucial balanced growth relationship in this context will be between the agricultural sector and the consumers' goods manufacturing sector. This approximates to the version (a) of the balanced growth theory in the last chapter. On the other hand, we may rely mainly on the provision of capital goods such as irrigation, power and machinery, and of other inputs such as fertilizers and improved seeds to expand agricultural output. Depending on the type of technical complementarity we stress, the crucial balanced growth relationship

will be either between agriculture and social overhead investment (as in the version (b)) or between agriculture and the
capital goods sector approximating to what I termed the 'communist' model in the last chapter.

Formally, the difference between the two approaches appears
to be that the first stresses the interdependence on the demand
side and the second stresses the interdependence on the supply
side. But more fundamental differences are involved in emphasizing the balanced growth between agriculture and the consumers' goods sector as contrasted with that between agriculture and the capital goods sector. They involve different
attitudes towards the use of positive economic incentives or the
use of compulsive economic pressures; and towards present
consumption or the future rate of economic growth.

If we are thinking of using positive economic incentives to
induce the farmers to produce a larger marketable surplus of
agriculture, then the conventional distinction between 'consumers' goods' and 'capital goods' is rather blurred. In so far
as food is necessary for the expansion of the manufacturing
sector, it is as much a 'capital good' as durable machinery: the
classical concept of capital as the 'subsistence fund' required to
maintain the workers during a time-involving process of production is still applicable. But granted this, the supply of manufactured consumers' goods which is necessary in order to induce
the farmers to produce a larger marketable surplus of food may
be regarded as much a 'capital good' as the direct physical inputs into agriculture. This is of course not to deny the importance of the essential physical inputs and capital goods in increasing agricultural output; but only to point out that the
mere physical provision of these inputs and capital goods need
not result in a larger supply of food surplus unless economic
incentives are created for the farmers to make full use of them.
Hence the crucial importance of the balanced growth between
agriculture and the manufactured consumers' goods sector.

Those who favour the second approach will argue, however, that to try to expand the output of the agricultural sector by using purely positive economic incentives may not be effective and is a very socially costly approach for a poor country. In trying to offer economic incentives, we are merely acquiescing in the farmers' unwillingness to postpone present consumption for the sake of faster future economic growth. With the limited resources of the manufacturing sector, expansion of the consumers' goods sector can take place only at the expense of the capital goods sector. Since economies of scale and technical complementarities are more important in the capital goods sector than in the consumers' goods sector, the attempt to maintain a balanced growth on the demand side between agriculture and the consumers' goods sector will therefore slow down the overall growth rate of the economy. They would prefer a considerable use of negative pressures to make a forcible collection of the agricultural surplus through taxation or compulsory collection of produce combined with the provision of the necessary inputs such as fertilizers, seeds or irrigation, for example.

In so far as we can judge from the experiences of the underdeveloped countries, neither the first nor the second approach is likely to succeed on its own, and the practical problem is to try to find an effective combination of the two which will suit local circumstances. In Chapter 3, we have seen that peasants do respond vigorously to positive economic incentives, but, under conditions of unaided free market conditions, much of the expansion in their output has been the result of bringing more land under cultivation rather than of improving agricultural productivity. On the other hand, the overpopulated countries can only expand their agricultural output by improving their agricultural productivity. In order to bring about changes in agricultural techniques and organization, the incentive approach needs to be supplemented by a variety of other measures ranging from improvements in irrigation and transport, in agricultural credit, marketing and extension services, to the provision of fertilizers and improved seeds. But this does not mean that a forcible extraction of the agricultural surplus through taxation or compulsory collection of agricultural produce on the 'communist' model is likely to work. This method has not been particularly successful even in Soviet Russia which in contrast to the overpopulated countries of today started out as a considerable exporter of wheat and still has a considerable amount of unused land. A country like India simply does not possess an 'agricultural surplus' in the Russian sense which may be forcibly collected. All we have got is the optical illusion of the 'concealed saving potential' based on the misconception that, because the marginal product of labour in overcrowded subsistence agriculture is zero, the surplus labour can be removed without reducing total output, thus automatically creating a food surplus to be extracted by taxation and compulsion. But as we have seen, the total agricultural output is likely to decline unless those who are left behind on the land are given positive economic incentives to work harder and to adopt more productive methods of cultivation. It is not inconceivable that beyond a certain point the attempt to pursue a forcible method of collecting the agricultural surplus may well drive the peasants into producing no surplus at all.

The way market incentives may be combined with government action in reforming agriculture and providing the necessary social overhead capital and other agricultural inputs may be illustrated by recent developments in Indian agriculture. During the decade 1950–60, the volume of Indian agricultural output, both food grains and other crops, seems to have risen by 45·5%, giving an annual rate of increase of about 4·5% or about twice the rate of population growth. (Since 1960, the Indian agricultural expansion seems to have tapered off.) This expansion has been the combined result of government land reforms, trying to eliminate the absentee landlords and other intermediaries, putting a ceiling on the acreage of land owner-ship and encouraging and enforcing the cultivation of land by owners; and of government assistance to agriculture through irrigation schemes and provision of fertilizers, improved seeds, dissemination of improved methods of cultivation, and other measures. But the most remarkable development has been the rise of commercial and even 'capitalist' agriculture, with indi-vidual holdings ranging from 10 to 50 acres, employing wage labour instead of family labour and using improved methods of cultivation and an increasing amount of capital. This type of farming now takes up about 65% of the total area under cultivation. This not only provides a dramatic contrast to the traditional picture of Indian agriculture with overcrowded sub-optimal holdings of 5 acres or less with heavy 'disguised unem-ployment' but also seems to be the main source (other than the extension of the cultivated area) of the expansion in the total agricultural output. As we have seen in Chapter 3, overpopula-tion on land leaves the peasants with little or no margin above their minimum subsistence level, and because of this lack of margin to face risks they tend to be inhibited from entering the money economy under unaided free market conditions. It has needed the Indian Government's land reforms to break down a part of this obstacle. These reforms have induced the hitherto absentee landlords to become active cultivators of their land and in some cases the compensation they received for the com-pulsory transfer of a part of their holding above the permitted ceiling provided them with the capital to invest on their remain-ing land. In some cases also, where the ceiling was too low for economic farming, some of the larger farmers have leased land from the small land owners; the small land owners now com-bine rent from their small-holdings with other occupations, thus becoming 'absentee landlords' in their turn. The larger commercialized farms may be regarded as the main source of the expanding marketable surplus of agricultural produce, for they have benefited most from the government's attempt to assist agriculture directly through the provision of irrigation, fertilizers, and other capital goods. Indeed, had the older pattern of subsistence farming persisted over the bulk of the agricultural sector, it is doubtful whether the government's attempt to inject the essential capital goods and input into the agricultural sector would have yielded much result.[1]

Choice of techniques and the choice between present and future

So far, we have been considering the choice between present consumption and future rate of growth in terms of the choice between expanding the consumers' goods sector or the capital goods sector to stimulate a corresponding expansion in the agricultural sector. But even when it is decided how much of the different types of goods should be produced, the problem of choice between the different time-paths of the income stream still remains. It now appears in the form of the choice between different methods of producing the same type of goods. Thus, in an overpopulated country suffering from a shortage of capital and land, should we not always choose the most labour-intensive method of producing a given commodity which combines the greatest possible quantity of the abundant factor—labour—to a given unit of scarce factor—capital or land? Under what conditions should we depart from this apparently commonsensical rule? Part of the answer to this question depends on our choice between present and future consumption.

To some extent, the question of the correct choice of techniques stated in terms of two factors of production such as labour and capital is oversimplified and artificial. In an actual situation, the choice depends not only on two selected factors

1. See *Seminar*, 38, on Indian Agriculture, New Delhi, October 1962; also S. C. Gupta, 'Some Aspects of Indian Agriculture', *Enquiry*, 6, New Delhi.

but on a variety of other things, notably the third main factor —skilled labour. Many underdeveloped countries suffer from a greater shortage of skills than of material capital, so that they sometimes prefer more expensive machinery, which reduces repairs and maintenance, to cheaper or second-hand machinery which, although it might reduce the ratio of capital to unskilled labour, requires a larger amount of the scarcest factor, skilled labour. Similarly, the machines which the underdeveloped countries can import are designed for the conditions in the advanced countries and are frequently too complicated and labour-saving for their own requirements. But these machines are produced in large numbers according to standard specifications and to try to alter them to suit the local conditions in the underdeveloped countries may make them a great deal more expensive than the standard article. Thus, in a wide range of modern manufacturing industry, the underdeveloped countries may have little choice but to buy the standard machines which are available in the market and, in most cases, to employ foreign technicians to run them. All they can do, in suitable cases, is to try to have multiple shifts of labour on a particular machine.

In spite of this, however, it is instructive to study the problem of the choice of techniques in relation to an overpopulated country such as India. For this has relevance not only to the relation between labour-intensive handicraft industries and modern factories in the consumers' goods sector, but also to the different methods of providing social overhead capital such as irrigation and transport. And, most interestingly in the light of my previous analysis, it has a great relevance also to the question of change-over from subsistence to commercial agriculture. Furthermore, the question of the choice of techniques leads us via the choice between present consumption and future economic growth to the equally fundamental choice between greater economic equality and faster economic growth.

At the end of Chapter 6, I said that beyond the problem of

finding the total capital requirements to produce a target output of a particular commodity on the basis of a given sectoral capital-output ratio, it is necessary to consider whether this ratio represents the most economical way of producing this commodity. At first sight, it may appear that to economize capital, we have merely to compare the different capital-output ratios required in the different methods of producing the same commodity, and choose the method with the lowest capital-output ratio. This is of course another way of saying that we should pick the method which produces the highest value of output per unit of capital. But this ignores the fact that, in addition to capital, labour is required to produce the commodity. So to find out the net value of output per unit of capital, we should take the gross value of output, and deduct the total labour cost of that output—measuring the total labour costs by the number of labour units required multiplied by the given money wage rate.

I can now state the bare bones of the problem of the choice of techniques. Some methods of producing a particular commodity are labour-intensive—they require a large quantity of labour in combination with a given unit of capital. But because of this, the labour costs in these methods are relatively high and they may therefore yield a comparatively low net output per unit of capital after the labour costs are deducted. These methods are typified by the handicraft and cottage industry methods of producing consumers' goods, and the spade-and-bucket method of constructing roads and irrigation works. On the other hand, there are the capital-intensive or labour-saving methods of producing a particular commodity, typified by the modern factory methods of producing consumers' goods, and mechanized methods of constructing roads, irrigation works and other projects. Here, because of lower labour costs and higher productivity, the net output per unit of capital may be comparatively high.

The advantage of the more labour intensive techniques is that for a given amount of capital investment they create a larger volume of employment. Since most of the wage income is spent on consumption, there is therefore a higher level of present consumption. Since a larger volume of employment means that the available income is spread over a larger number of people, there is also a higher degree of economic equality. On the other hand, the advantage of the more capital-intensive methods is, that for a given amount of capital investment, they yield a higher net output or surplus above the wage bill; this surplus can be made available for further investment. So although they yield a lower volume of present employment and consumption, they promise a higher rate of economic growth in the future, and therefore a higher potential level of employment and consumption in the future. There is, however, a greater degree of unequal distribution of income between the (state or private) 'capitalists' who obtain the surplus and the wage earners, and also between those workers who obtain immediate employment and those who for the present are left unabsorbed in the productive process.

The same analysis applies to the changeover from subsistence agriculture to commercial and 'capitalist' agriculture; the only modification is that we have to treat land as the most important form of the scarce factor, capital. Subsistence farming provides the greatest volume of employment, 'disguised' or otherwise, for a given land area. Even when the 'disguised' unemployment is removed, so that those who remain on the land put in a 'full day's work', subsistence farming still represents the most labour-intensive way of cultivating a particular crop so long as family labour instead of wage labour is used. This is so because in this type of farming the aim is to maximize the total output which can be squeezed out of the family holding; and since labour is free within the family, it will be applied to a particular piece of land until the marginal product of the last unit of labour falls to zero. Once the system of wage labour is introduced, labour-intensity per unit of land will decline even if the technique of cultivation remains the same as before, say by bullocks and ploughs. This is so because the employer of agricultural labour will only apply it up to the point where the marginal product of the last unit of labour is equal to its wage rate.

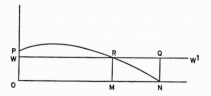

This can be easily seen in the above diagram, where the marginal product of labour is measured on the vertical axis and the number of units of labour (and not workers) is measured on the horizontal axis. Under subsistence farming ON units of labour will be applied to a given piece of land with given technique and capital equipment. This gives a maximum total food output of PNO from the given area of land. Let OW be the wage (in terms of the food crop) per unit of labour. Under commercial farming, producing the same crop with the same technique of cultivation and capital equipment, only OM units of labour will be applied to the same piece of land; for at this point the marginal product of the last unit of labour MR is equal to its wage rate. Compared to subsistence agriculture, therefore, the ratio of labour to land is reduced under commercial agriculture. So is the gross total output PRMO which is less than that of subsistence agriculture, PNO. But the net marketable surplus measured by PRW will be increased under commercial agriculture. Assume that under both systems of agriculture, the wage rate OW represents the food consumption per unit of labour (as distinct from per worker). Under subsistence farmng, the total retained consumption on the farm is WQNO and f this is equal to the total production PNO, there will be no marketable surplus. But under commercial agriculture, the removal of MN units of labour from the farm, which before were consuming RQNM amount of food, will raise the marketable food surplus by RQN. This is equal to PRW, assuming that there was no marketable surplus before. But in practice, the marketable surplus is likely to be larger since commercial agriculture is generally more efficient. The reason for this is that a part of the cash income from it can be used for buying fertilizers and improved seeds and for leasing extra units of land to increase the size of the holding to the optimum, making full use of the existing capital equipment. In many Asian countries, the optimum size of the farm with a pair of bullocks and a plough is about ten acres, which is larger than the average size of their subsistence farms.

Now if we were concerned with obtaining the highest present consumption of food in purely physical terms, irrespective of who consumed it and where, then subsistence agriculture would represent a 'superior' method. But the advantage of commercial agriculture with a higher marketable food surplus is that the surplus can be used not merely as retained consumption on the farms, but anywhere in the economy where it is most needed for future economic growth—to feed those in the consumers' goods industries, or capital goods industries or in the construction of social overhead capital.

In the Asian conditions, the different degrees of labour-intensity in agriculture may be illustrated in terms of the three main types of cultivation. Firstly, there is the traditional subsistence agriculture. This represents the highest level of present consumption and also provides a sort of social security system for the largest number of people on a given land area. But, unfortunately, it represents agricultural stagnation aggravated by population pressure and offers nothing for future growth.

Next, we have commercial agriculture with wage labour, but still using the most labour-intensive method of cultivation represented by a pair of bullocks and plough. Finally, we have mechanized farming on the basis of larger holdings using tractors and combine harvesters, involving the largest amount of removal or eviction of labour from land. When people talk about 'land reform', they sometimes mean the breaking up of larger estates and redistribution of the land to landless peasants. This implies choosing the first or second alternative, and increasing population pressure is likely to make it into a return to subsistence agriculture. Sometimes, 'land reform' is used in the opposite sense, that of consolidating the smaller peasant holdings into bigger 'collective' or 'co-operative' farms using tractors and other capital-intensive methods. This implies a more ruthless method of evicting people from land and trying to extract a larger agricultural surplus in the hope of a faster rate of future economic growth.

The upshot of recent discussions[1] on the choice of techniques has been to show that it is not possible to make an invariable choice in favour of more labour-intensive techniques even in overpopulated countries, unless we make explicit choices between present and future. The more we value raising the present level of consumption and employment against future growth, the more we should favour labour-intensive techniques. The 'commonsense' view that overpopulated countries should always prefer labour-intensive methods conceals an implicit preference for present over future, and represents a very short 'planning horizon'. On the longer 'planning horizon', the more we value the future rate of growth over the present level of consumption and employment, the more we should favour capital intensive methods which are capable of yielding a larger surplus of output over wage costs for a given capital outlay and so make possible a higher rate of re-investment for the future.

1. Cf. A. K. Sen, *Choice of Techniques*, particularly Chs. 2 and 5.

Forced saving and deficit financing

I shall now return to the central issues of the balanced growth path theory. We have seen that the overall rate of growth for the economy will be determined by the rate of growth of its slowest moving sector, agriculture. To try to stimulate the output of the agricultural sector by using only positive economic incentives may be effective, but this means diverting a considerable part of the resources of the manufacturing sector from the capital goods sector to the consumers' goods sector, and slowing down the rate of growth. On the other hand, however, to try to use negative pressures such as taxation or compulsory collection of produce may also lead to a 'peasants' strike', resulting in a lesser amount of agricultural surplus, and slowing down the rate of growth. In this situation, many economists have toyed with the idea of accelerating economic growth by deficit financing which would facilitate the transfer of 'disguised unemployment' from agriculture into productive work, particularly in the construction of social overhead capital such as irrigation projects or roads. They also argue that this type of deficit financing may be pursued without serious long-term consequences since the inflation which it creates will be 'self-destroying'—because when the capital projects are completed they will add to the output of agriculture and other consumers' goods.

This is altogether different from saying that the social cost of making use of the 'disguised unemployment' is zero. On the contrary, it is recognized that there is a genuine social cost in doing so in the form of extra consumption by the workers on the capital projects, who will spend most of their wages on food and other consumers' goods. In fact, deficit financing is called for because this extra consumption cannot be met out of taxation and voluntary saving, so that 'forced saving' has to be imposed through inflation. So while the workers on the capital projects are able to command a larger share of real income through the increase in money incomes, the farmers, for instance, will find that they have been obliged to cut down their level of consumption through the rise in the prices of the consumers' goods that they wish to buy.

The idea that inflation will be self-destroying is based on the assumption that the extra money income created by deficit financing will become *stabilized* at a certain level, so that after a time-lag, the extra output of consumers' goods which result from the new capital goods can catch up with it.[1] This in turn is based on the Keynesian Multiplier theory and the assumption of stable marginal propensity to save and consume. In the original Keynesian context, we start from a situation of depression where both labour and the productive capacity which goes with it are unemployed. Deficit financing, therefore, will merely expand employment and output without raising prices of consumers' goods whose output can be expanded directly. Given stable prices, then it is reasonable to assume that at each round the people who receive the extra income will go on saving and spending in certain stable proportions as before; and so long as a certain proportion of income is saved each round—that is, so long as the marginal propensity to consume is less than 1—then the total resultant income will converge towards a stable equilibrium level. In the underdeveloped countries, however, we start from a situation with only surplus labour without the necessary productive equipment to go with it. So surplus labour can at best produce some extra capital goods which only after a time-lag can produce consumers' goods. Immediately, therefore, the prices of consumers' goods must go up. How far this inflation will be self-destroying depends on how far the people in the under-

1. W. A. Lewis, 'Economic Development with Unlimited Supplies of Labour', *The Manchester School*, May 1954.

developed countries who receive the extra money income will go on saving and spending it in stable proportions in the face of the rising prices of consumers' goods.

In the underdeveloped countries which have just emerged from the orthodox monetary conditions typified by the 100% Sterling Standard, people may still retain some confidence in money and hold to the 'illusion' that its value will continue to be the same as before. The posthumous benefit of this maligned orthodox monetary system is that it provides the newly independent monetary authorities with some scope for deficit financing without upsetting confidence. But as prices continue to rise, the marginal propensity to consume, which started very high in any case, will tend towards 1. For one thing, rising costs of living will compel people to spend most of their income and reduce their saving, and even borrow for consumption purposes. For another thing, as soon as people expect that prices will go on rising, they will become increasingly disinclined to save any part of their money income, since this form of saving will be quickly depreciating in value. They will increasingly tend to spend all their money income as quickly as possible by hoarding food and other consumers' goods, or by buying gold, jewellery and real estate whose value keeps up with rising prices. Once this gathers momentum, money incomes will not be stabilized at a certain level in the Keynesian manner; instead we shall be back in the world of the Quantity Theory where the total volume of purchasing power is increased at each round as the original sum of money is multiplied by its quickening velocity of circulation. The rising cost of living will lead to demands for higher money wages, and if they are conceded we shall have the familiar wage-price spiral. In these conditions it seems very difficult to believe that inflation will be self-destroying, and this pessimism is confirmed by the typical monetary conditions in underdeveloped countries which are marked by the continual tendency to boil over into

K

further bouts of rising prices or tighter foreign exchange controls to meet the balance of payments crises.[1]

To sum up: there is no simple short cut to increasing the agricultural surplus without trying to tackle the difficult problem of raising agricultural productivity. The merit of the balanced growth path theory is to show that the overall rate of growth of a (closed) economy cannot be sustained without a simultaneous expansion in its slowest moving sector—agriculture. This basic 'balanced growth' relation arises from the fact that the size of the agricultural surplus forms the 'subsistence fund' required to support the workers during the waiting period before the result of their labour becomes available in the form of final output. The larger the size of its agricultural surplus, the longer a society can afford to wait for the fruits of capital investment, and the more elaborate the type of capital investment it can afford to undertake. The role of the *marketable* surplus is that it helps to move the food surplus of the farms to other parts of the economy where they may be able to contribute more to future economic growth. It is the tragedy of the overpopulated countries that while they need a faster rate of growth to relieve population pressure, they have a smaller potential food surplus above minimum subsistence consumption to be used for this purpose. If they are too poor to rely on positive economic incentives to induce the farmers to grow more food, they do not possess a large potential agricultural surplus which can be extracted by coercive methods, by taxation and by forced saving. This basic fact has been obscured by the misconception that compared with the thinly populated underdeveloped countries, the overpopulated countries have a greater 'concealed saving potential' in the form of their 'disguised unemployment'.

1. Cf. M. Bronfenbrenner, 'The High Cost of Economic Development', *Land Economics*, August 1953.

9

International Trade and Economic Development

I shall now leave the closed economy and consider the implications of the balanced growth path theory for the developing countries which have a high ratio of export to national income and are not yet suffering from population pressure.

With international trade, it is clear that a country need not try to maintain an internal balanced growth relation between the different sectors of its domestic economy. It may produce some commodities in excess of its domestic requirements and export them, and in return import commodities for which its requirements exceed domestic production. Indeed, it is the aim of the traditional free trade theory to show that correcting domestic imbalances through exports and imports is preferable to maintaining a strict balanced growth relationship within a self-sufficient economy, since it enables the country to enjoy the advantages of international specialization according to comparative costs.

The traditional free trade position has been challenged in two ways. Firstly, at a semi-popular level, there is the complaint of those developing countries with a high ratio of export to national income that their past pattern of economic development, encouraging the export sector at the expense of the domestic sector, is 'lop-sided' and 'unbalanced' and that this fundamental imbalance should be cured by an all-out attempt to foster the domestic manufacturing sector.

This argument has considerable weight in so far as it relates to the need for reducing the vulnerability of the underdeveloped 'export economies' to the violent price fluctuations of primary products in the world market. There are no disagreements in principle about this point, but the practical difficulties of organizing effective and acceptable commodity stabilization schemes have not been overcome. Many commodity schemes flounder in the conflict of short-run national interests between the producing and the consuming countries, even where it is recognized that both parties may benefit from the schemes in the long run. Thus, in spite of various proposals, ranging from commodity agreements or international buffer stock schemes, etc., to international monetary plans to stabilize the flow of short-run funds and ease international liquidity, there have been meagre practical results in this field of international co-operation.

The special difficulties of the underdeveloped countries arise, not only from the high ratio of exports to national income, but also from lack of flexibility in their production structure to respond to changes in the terms of trade between their exports and their imports. Unlike the industrially advanced export economies, these countries cannot easily switch from one line of export to another. Moreover, while the industrially advanced export economies normally have a considerable home market for their major lines of manufactured exports, the underdeveloped export economies do not have much of a home market for their major lines of primary exports to absorb the surplus when the world market conditions turn against these products. Given the same ratio of export to national income, therefore, an underdeveloped export economy is likely to suffer more from a fluctuation in world market prices than an industrially advanced export economy. Ideally, of course, the underdeveloped countries should try to attain a greater flexibility and adaptability in their production structure by expanding their domestic manufacturing sector *without* reducing their export sector and its potential rate of growth. In practice, many countries find it difficult to build up a domestic manufacturing sector without robbing a considerable amount of capital and technical resources from the export sector, and frequently the export sector merely degenerates into a convenient source of foreign exchange to finance the domestic industrial sector. So with the present unsatisfactory state of international co-operation, to reduce short-run instabilities in the prices of primary exports the underdeveloped countries will have to make a painful choice between higher income from greater specialization in export commodities and a greater degree of insulation against the vagaries of the world market. How far they should pursue the second aim will depend on the particular circumstances of individual countries. What they should avoid is a wholesale reaction against primary exports in favour of domestic manufacturing industries without a clear appreciation of the full implications of the choice they are making.

Once we pass from the problems of short-term economic instability to those of long-term economic development, the notion of 'unbalanced growth' created by a high ratio of export to national income becomes less justifiable. Prima facie, there is no good reason for saying that a country with a higher ratio of export to national income must necessarily suffer from a greater degree of unbalanced growth. It all depends on our judgement of the possibilities of expanding the demand for and the supply of output of the different sectors in existing proportions. It is perfectly possible for a country with a high ratio of export to national income to go on expanding steadily provided there is a steady rate of growth of demand for its export products, and provided it can go on supplying them without rising costs. This leads us to the second line of attack on the traditional free trade theory, this time conducted at a more sophisticated level by some of the balanced growth economists, notably Professor Nurkse.[1]

Declining world demand for primary products?

Professor Nurkse accepts the benefits of international specialization based on comparative costs, but he argues that for the purpose of economic growth, the relevant question is not whether countries should specialize according to the existing international demand for their products, but whether this demand is likely to go on expanding in future. He also accepts that in the past international trade has acted as the engine of growth, by serving as the medium through which the industrial centres of the world in Western Europe transmitted their economic growth to the periphery of the underdeveloped countries, through a vigorous expansion of demand for primary products. But he argues that this nineteenth-century mechanism, from which the newly settled regions of North America and Australasia particularly benefited, is no longer available to the present-day underdeveloped countries of the tropics. Instead of the United Kingdom and Western Europe, the world's industrial centre has now shifted to the United States which, with its abundant natural resources and great size, has a relatively lesser need to import primary products. Further, there are the trend factors, such as the low income elasticity of demand for primary products, the change in the industrial structure of the advanced countries from light industries to heavy engineering and chemical industries with a lower raw material requirement, the invention of synthetic substitutes for natural raw materials and the agricultural protection in the advanced countries. Even if there were no

1. Cf. R. Nurkse, *Patterns of World Trade and Development*, Wicksell Lectures, 1959, and *The Conflict between 'Balanced Growth' and International Specialization*, Istanbul and Ankara.

difficulties from the supply side created by diminishing returns, it is not sensible for the underdeveloped countries to go on specializing in primary products in the face of a declining trend in the world market demand for them. Rather, they should look to the development of the domestic manufacturing sector as the alternative engine of growth to international trade.

Professor Nurkse's argument has a number of weaknesses which it shares with other predictions[1] about the unfavourable long-term trend in the world demand for primary products that have been put forward from time to time.

First, we should remind ourselves that the underdeveloped countries produce only a part of the total world's exports of primary products, so that it is not always safe to regard them as identical with 'primary exporters'. For instance, one of the adverse factors which Professor Nurkse mentions—agricultural protection in the European countries—mainly affects the temperate zone products. With the notable exception of sugar, the tropical underdeveloped countries are not affected by it.

Secondly, most of these predictions are made by lumping different types of primary products into one general category. This conceals considerable differences in the trend of demand for different commodities. During any given period, the fortunes of the underdeveloped countries exporting different commodities will of course depend a great deal on the 'luck of the draw'; those supplying the stagnant and declining manufacturing industries having to face an equally stagnant demand, and those supplying new and expanding manufacturing industries enjoying buoyant demand. At certain periods in the nineteenth century, for example, the rise of the textile industries created an expanding demand for raw cotton, and in the post-

I. e.g. the United Nations Reports on the *Relative Prices of Exports and Imports of the Underdeveloped Countries*, 1949, and *Economic Development of Latin America*, 1950. For further details see T. Morgan, 'The Long-Run Terms of Trade Between Agriculture and Manufacturing', *Economic Development and Cultural Change*, October 1959.

war period, the rise of the motor industry has created a strong demand for petroleum and, to a lesser extent, rubber. Professor Nurkse somehow regards the post-war boom in petroleum as an exception to the general rule, but this seems somewhat arbitrary in the longer-run historical perspective. It is of course difficult for the underdeveloped countries which do not possess oil and cannot readily shift from a stagnant line of primary export to another with a greater demand prospect. But this is not the same as saying that the nineteenth-century mechanism of the transmission of growth through international trade has ceased to work for all primary exporters.

Thirdly, we should take into account the two major changes which are taking place within the developing countries themselves. The first is the growth of the domestic consumers' goods industries gradually substituting imports. It has been estimated that the developing countries now import only about a third of their total consumption of manufactures, producing the remaining two-thirds at home.[1] This rise of light industries in the developing countries should generate a new demand for raw materials to offset to some extent the declining demand from the advanced countries due to greater economies in the use of the raw materials and the shift of the industrial structure to heavy engineering and chemical products with a lower raw-material content. The second factor is of course the 'population explosion' in the underdeveloped countries which, even given the limitations of purchasing power, is bound to exert an upward pressure on the demand for food.

The arguments above in which I have marshalled the favourable factors for the future world demand for primary products are no more or no less convincing than the adverse factors which Professor Nurkse has pointed out. This is so because I have left out one decisive factor from the analysis— price. Professor Nurkse, like other balanced growth theorists,

1. *International Trade, 1959*, GATT, 1960, p. 14.

tends to concentrate too much on income elasticities of demand, neglecting the vital factor of relative costs and prices. For instance, he tends to look upon the nineteenth-century expansion of world trade in primary products as though it simply sprang from the overflow of demand in the industrial countries. But, as Professor Cairncross has pointed out, that process depended also on the power of the overseas primary producers to capture a larger *share* of the market in Western Europe, and particularly the United Kingdom, by being *low-cost producers*. By the same token, if the present-day underdeveloped countries wish to capture a larger share of the world market in primary products, they will have to regain their position as low-cost producers. Making use of calculations by Mr. Alfred Maizels of the National Institute of Economic and Social Research, Professor Cairncross shows how the price factor seems to have influenced the share of the world exports in primary products between the underdeveloped countries and the industrial countries: 'In 1937 the volume of primary produce from the industrial countries was slightly lower than in 1913 while exports from non-industrial countries were over 50% higher. Unit export values had climbed about 10% for the industrial countries and fallen slightly for others. By 1950, there had been a spectacular change. Exports from the industrial countries had increased while exports from other countries had fallen sharply. At the same time, while the unit values doubled for the first group they more than trebled for the second. In 1957 both groups had added 50% to the volume of their exports of primary produce and the divergence in unit value had narrowed only slightly.'

From these calculations, Professor Cairncross concludes that the reason the underdeveloped countries have made less headway than the industrial countries since 1937 and no greater headway even since 1950 is not the general sluggishness of world demand for primary exports; in fact both groups enjoyed a 50% expansion in the volume of exports in the seven years 1950–7. The reason must be found in the failure of the underdeveloped countries as a group to reduce the prices of their primary exports in relation to the primary exports from the industrial countries.[1]

The price factor again is very important in getting a proper perspective on one powerful factor adversely affecting the world demand for primary products—the substitution of raw materials by synthetic products. The invention or the commercial exploitation of these synthetic substitutes is not simply brought about by an autonomous general advance of technology unconnected with price and cost factors. More often than not, it is induced by abnormal scarcity and high prices of a particular natural product. For instance, synthetic rubber was introduced during the Second World War because natural rubber from South-East Asia was not available. In the post-war period, the ability of Malaya to hold her competitive position against synthetic rubber by improved methods and replanting is significant. At first sight, one might imagine that the superior modern technology of the synthetic rubber producers in the United States would get the better of the natural rubber producers in Malaya. But it is the point of the theory of comparative costs, properly interpreted as a dynamic process of productive adaptation, that this need not be so. The United States may have a general technological superiority over Malaya, but provided Malaya applies sufficient capital and modern technology to improving her rubber production, there is no reason why she should not be able to hold on to her comparative advantage in the production of that *particular*

1. A. K. Cairncross, *Factors in Economic Development*, pp. 200–2. In addition to the price factor, we should take into account the important effect of wartime disruption on the export trade of the underdeveloped countries caused by shortages in shipping and materials, and in South-East Asia by the destruction of physical capital through fighting and denial policy.

commodity. Conversely, the underdeveloped countries can lose their comparative advantage in their traditional lines of exports if they are unwilling to plough back sufficient capital and technical resources into their export production, and if they use their export sector merely as a milch cow to finance their domestic manufacturing sector. For instance, one might have imagined that the position of the South-East Asian rice exporting countries would be uniformly rosy, given the tremendous growth of the rice-consuming population in Asia. Yet in the post-war years some of them have suffered a set-back, because the government policy of starving agriculture in favour of manufacturing industry has resulted in the slow recovery to the pre-war levels of output of rice and a failure to reduce its price. This has led some of the Indian consumers to substitute wheat from the richer primary exporting countries for rice, and to some extent there has been a permanent shift of consumers' tastes from rice to wheat. Ironically, the United States free gifts of surplus wheat to India have also aggravated the difficulties of the South-East Asian rice exporters.

Let us now turn from the demand to the supply side of the argument that the underdeveloped countries should not go on specializing and expanding the output of their primary exports. This is based on the familiar view that, unlike manufacturing industry, primary production is subject to diminishing returns. A self-sustained process of economic development cannot therefore be built on the expansion of primary exports, since this will come to a stop sooner or later when suitable natural resources have been fully brought into use, or are exhausted, as in mining, for example. There is some justification for this fear in the case of mining, although even here it may be noted that some of the mining export economies have been able to prolong their growth by a more intensive application of capital and technical knowledge to the search for new sources of minerals and new methods of processing. When we come to other types of exports, the question whether the expansion can be sustained depends not on whether a particular line of export is a primary product or a manufactured product, but on whether technical improvements can be introduced to raise productivity and reduce costs. Even well-established exporters of manufactured products cannot escape stagnation when they fail to improve productivity and reduce costs in their export production.

In Chapters 3 and 4, we have seen that the past pattern of export expansion in many underdeveloped countries has been characterized by low productivity and technical stagnation. The peasant export sector has expanded simply by bringing more land under cultivation without any significant change in traditional agricultural methods. The mining and plantation sector could have become the spearhead of modern technology and improved methods, but it has been crippled first by its cheap labour policy of low wages and low productivity, and more recently, by nationalistic reactions in the newly independent countries against foreign enterprise. These tend to discourage the new investment that is necessary to raise long-run productivity. With this failure to improve technical efficiency, it is no wonder that the expansion in primary export production is likely to come up against diminishing returns. But given the same condition of inefficient and stagnant technology, there is an equally severe limit to the expansion of domestic manufacturing industry through import-substitution, as many of the developing countries are now beginning to find.

Limits to import substitution

The manufacturing industries of the developing countries are typically light consumers' goods industries produced on the basis of borrowed technology. They import the machinery, technicians and frequently a large part of their semi-processed materials from abroad, and many of them are limited to assembling, packaging and giving 'finishing touches' to the final products with a very high import-content. In a large number of them, technical efficiency is low, and they require heavy and prolonged protection against their foreign competitors. In these conditions, the rate of growth of the domestic manufacturing sector is decided by the size of the local market for each of the imported goods in relation to the output of the smallest sized factory which can be set up to produce it. To begin with, the import substitution may be quite quick, as the imports with large ready-made local markets are taken over and diverted to local producers through import restrictions. But after a time, this process will come to a stop. First, the size of the market for the remaining imports will get progressively smaller in relation to the minimum efficient units of production, setting up a limit on the demand side. Secondly, the available foreign exchange supply will have been depleted in the payments for the imported machinery, tecnicians and materials required for the new industries, and we come up against the familiar foreign exchange bottleneck and the balance of payments problem.

Alternative trade policies

Theoretically, there are three possible ways out of the impasse: (i) to expand the foreign exchange earnings from primary products; (ii) to cut down the import content of the domestic consumers' goods industries by setting up domestic capital goods industries; and (iii) to try to export manufactured goods. In practice, none of these policies are easy to achieve and all of them require considerable improvements in technical efficiency.

At one extreme, there are those countries, a majority of the export economies in Latin America, South-East Asia and Africa, which are not yet suffering from significant population pressure on their natural resources, and which moreover are relatively small in geographical area and population. For this type of country, the first alternative would seem to be the most promising. As we have seen, their past pattern of primary export expansion has been based on backward and stagnant technology and organization which still leaves very obvious scope for improvement by applying more capital and technical resources. Moreover, the overall size of their economies are generally too small for setting up domestic capital goods industries. Malaya is a good example of a country trying this route to further development.

At the other extreme, there are a few large countries such as India which are overpopulated, with a low ratio of export to national income. It is generally agreed that the first alternative does not seem very promising for these countries. On the other hand, their large overall size offers a promising basis for setting up domestic capital goods industries which are dependent on the economies of scale. They would have to combine this policy of more intensive import-substitution with the third alternative of trying to develop export industries in manufactures. Professor Nurkse's balanced growth approach seems most applicable to these countries.

Among the intermediate cases, the most unfortunate ones seem to be the small overpopulated island economies such as Ceylon and Mauritius. They are too densely populated to hope for further significant expansion of their existing primary exports, and they are too small to follow a massive industrialization policy suitable for larger countries. Some special cases such as Hong Kong and Puerto Rico have been able to obtain relief through exporting labour-intensive manufactured goods, but it is doubtful whether this solution will be generally available to others. Firstly, there are the political obstacles. For instance, it is doubtful whether a country like Ceylon will be able at present to follow either the pure free trade policy followed by Hong Kong or the special relationship with the United States developed by Puerto Rico. Secondly, there is a growing resistance on the part of the older industries in the advanced countries, for example the Lancashire Cotton industry, to the import of cheaper light consumers' goods from the developing countries such as Hong Kong and India. So instead of the agricultural protection mentioned by Professor Nurkse, the industrial protection on the part of the advanced countries against the light consumers' goods from the developing countries is a more serious obstacle to the growth of some of these countries.[1] Thirdly, the developing countries trying to export manufactured goods to the advanced countries have to contend with a serious further obstacle. In order to break into the market of the richer countries, the exports have to be high quality consumers' goods. On the other hand, it is difficult to produce such high quality products economically in the developing countries, not only because of their technical immaturity, but also because their domestic consumers are geared to the cheaper low quality products, so that they cannot hope to obtain the economies of scale based on the home market for these high quality products.

A new look at the free trade-protection controversy

The analysis I have just made adds a number of qualifications to the conventional discussion of free trade and protection in relation to the developing countries.

1. 'It is of *vital importance* that policy-makers in the mature countries should now be envisaging a state of affairs in the not-too-distant future in which a high proportion of their citizens' demand for "traditional products" are supplied from the developing countries overseas. But, whatever the policies of the mature countries, developing countries should aim at expanding their output of exportable manufactures at prices so competitive as to be able to surmount the protective barriers of those countries.' Sir Roy Harrod, 'Economic Development and Asian Regional Co-operation', *Pakistan Development Review*, Spring 1962, p. 4.

(i) The conventional discussion still runs in terms of a *horizontal* division of labour between the advanced countries producing manufactured goods and the developing countries producing primary products. But as we have seen, a considerable proportion of the world's primary exports is produced by the richer countries, while the developing countries produce about two-thirds of their consumption of manufactured goods. It is more interesting, therefore, to focus attention on the *vertical* international division of labour concerning the different stages in the production of the internationally traded goods. From the viewpoint of the developing countries, the interesting question is how far they can intensify their process of industrialization, either by pushing further back from the light 'finishing touches' industries to the manufacture of intermediate and capital goods or by processing their primary products a few stages further before exporting them.

(ii) A new conception of protection follows from this. Instead of protecting a single industry in isolation, we now have to think in terms of a whole group of industries. At present, the most common pattern of protection in the developing countries is protection 'in width', covering a horizontal group of light consumers' goods industries. In so far as these industries are chosen in a 'balanced' way according to the pattern of consumers' demand for them, this approximates to the version (a) of the balanced growth theory discussed in Chapter 7. Protection of the import-substitute industries by taking over the ready-made markets of the imports is an important method of overcoming the smallness in the size of the home market. But sooner or later, the possibilities of import-substitution in light consumers' goods industries will come to an end, and then we shall have to explore the possibilities of protection 'in depth', covering a vertical group of technically related industries at the different stages of production of a particular product: the possibility, for example, of extending protection in the textile industry from spinning and weaving to the manufacture of textile machinery. With the prevailing balanced growth philosophy of 'pushing ahead simultaneously on all fronts', many developing countries try to carry out, ineffectually, a protectionist policy both in width and depth. The interesting question is how far it is possible for them to push ahead more effectively with protection in depth in selected industries *by narrowing* the width of their protectionist policy.

(iii) In addition to the balanced growth theory, two further arguments have been used to justify the protection of manufacturing industry in the developing countries. The first springs from the notion that in the overpopulated countries, the social cost of labour is zero since 'disguised unemployment' can be removed from agriculture without reducing output. The manufacturing sector has, however, to pay labour at the prevailing money wages and so its private costs exceed the social costs of production and its output is below optimum. Hence protection to cure this deviation from the optimum allocation of resources. In the light of our analysis in Chapters 6 and 8, this argument will have to be rejected. We have seen that expanding employment in the manufacturing sector will lead to an extra demand for and consumption of food which is a very genuine social cost in a country with a limited supply of food. We have also seen that in order to obtain the same output from agriculture, after the 'disguised unemployment' is removed, those who remain on the land have to be provided with incentive consumers' goods to induce them to work harder and put in the same total amount of work on the land as before. With the limited resources, more consumers' goods can be provided only at the expense of cutting down the production of capital goods. So the process of inducing the farmers not to reduce their output and extracting the food surplus from the agricultural sector is also not socially costless.

L

Finally, the trouble with this particular argument for protection is that it can be applied to all cases of transfer of labour from the overcrowded subsistence economy to all types of wage-paying industry, including the mines and plantations!

(iv) The second argument for protection is the 'infant industry' argument, particularly in the form that the costs of the protected industry will be reduced after a period of 'learning process'. This has been conceded by the orthodox free trade theorists themselves and the modern writers on the developing countries have widened the argument to embrace the notion of the 'infant manufacturing sector' or, as some would have it, the 'infant economy'. In the light of our analysis, it may be questioned whether the dynamic 'educative' effect depends so simply on the differences between manufacturing industry and primary production. In the past, the mining and plantation sector has exerted little 'educative' effect on the indigenous people because of the cheap labour policy. But this should not blind us to the possibility that with suitable re-organization, the foreign-owned mining and plantation enterprises, where they are based on modern technology, heavy capital investment and modern methods of economic organization, can still exert a very valuable 'educative' effect on the developing countries. Conversely, the domestic manufacturing industries of the developing countries, when they are run inefficiently with limited capital and backward technology and on the urban equivalent of the cheap labour policy as symbolized by the shanty towns, cannot be expected to exert much 'educative' effect on the people. Frequently, the dynamic stimulating effects which some observers report near urban industrial sectors may be as much due to the spread of the exchange economy in the simple sense as to the rise of manufacturing industry.

(v) Finally, I should note one serious obstacle to the pursuit of an effective protectionist policy in most developing countries, and paradoxically this arises from their excessive use of import restrictions! With their attempt to strain forward with economic development plans inspired by the 'big push' and balanced growth theories, their investment programmes outstrip the resources they can mobilize with their existing financial and fiscal competence. This has subjected them to a continual pressure of internal inflation and external balance of payments difficulties requiring severe import controls. Typically, these are in the form of quantitative restrictions on imports introduced on an ad hoc basis with each round of balance of payments crises, and they have been allowed to spread indiscriminately over the entire foreign trade sector. The characteristic results are not only a rising general price level and an all-round premium on all imported goods, but also distorted price differentials between different types of imports haphazardly reflecting short-run and speculative factors. In a crisis situation which is continually threatening to boil over into a further round of import restrictions, government policy tends to be concerned with the short-term objective of trying to prevent too rapid a rise in the cost of living rather than with long-term development. But however broadly we may define it, a protectionist policy essentially remains a method of selective encouragement of some groups of industries over others and as I have said in (ii) above, the important question for many developing countries is how far they can effectively promote protection in depth along selected lines by narrowing the width of their protection. But this means that the differential advantage accorded to the protected industries, say in the higher prices for their products, should be maintained in sharp relief over a long period instead of being swamped by random rises in the prices of the other non-protected imports. Unfortunately, this is precisely what the developing countries cannot hope to ensure, in their existing situation of foreign exchange crises and financial instability. Thus, there is a conflict between an effective protectionist policy which resembles the 'unbalanced growth' approach, concentrating encouragement on selected strategic sectors, and the 'big push' cum-balanced-growth approach of pushing ahead simultaneously on all fronts.

10

Conclusions: General Issues of Development Policy

In this book I have set out to provide a balanced picture of the different types of underdeveloped country at different stages of development, and a systematic examination of the arguments behind the leading economic development policies of the post-war period.

Chapters 3, 4 and 5 cover the first part of my programme. In these chapters I have provided alternatives to the conventional model of an overpopulated country at a somewhat advanced stage of general development by focussing attention on the underdeveloped countries not suffering from population pressure and at earlier stages of general development. I was also concerned with the subjective problem of discontent as distinct from the problem of material poverty, and have analysed the process of export expansion in different settings in order to appraise the prevailing reaction against the 'colonial' or 'the nineteenth-century pattern' of economic development. The problems of 'dualistic' economic structure which I have outlined are of course not peculiar to the thinly populated underdeveloped countries. They are equally present in the overpopulated countries, and are frequently aggravated by population pressure. But I hope that these problems have stood out more sharply by being isolated from the problem of population pressure.

From Chapter 6 onwards I was concerned with the second

part of my programme. This has led me into a critical survey of the leading ideas behind the post-war policies of economic development, such as 'disguised unemployment', the overall capital-output ratio, the critical minimum size of the development programme and the various versions of the balanced growth theory. I have tried to show that frequently these ideas are extensions of the Keynesian and the post-Keynesian theoretical approach inappropriate to the underdeveloped countries. What I have done in effect was to bring to bear upon these modern ideas some of the relevant parts of the classical and neo-classical approach. For example, I have tried to show the weakness of the concept of a stable overall capital-output ratio in the light of the Ricardian theory. I have indicated the weakness of the balanced growth theory based on the income effect and set patterns of expansion in consumption and production in the light of the substitution effect and flexible patterns of consumption and production of the neo-classical analysis. I have tried in particular to show that when all has been said and done about the economies of scale, indivisibilities and complementarities, we cannot ultimately afford to ignore the problem of choice, for, beyond a certain point, different lines of economic development activity compete for the available scarce resources.

In Chapter 9, I have tried to combine the relevant parts of the older and newer theoretical approaches to consider how far the prevailing reaction against the so-called 'nineteenth-century pattern' of international trade is justified, and how far a policy of rapid and intensive industrialization based on heavy capital goods industries is appropriate in the different settings of the different types of underdeveloped country.

In this concluding section I shall bring out the implications of my analysis for some of the more general issues of development policy.

Dilemmas of development policy

It should by now be clear that it is not sufficient merely to say that the level of per capita incomes in the underdeveloped countries should be raised, without squarely facing some of the painful choices which are involved.

(i) There is the problem of choice between higher income and economic security. This has faced the people of the underdeveloped countries since the early stages of transition from the subsistence economy to the exchange economy, and culminates in the intractable problems of the instability and the vulnerability of the underdeveloped countries with a high ratio of export to national income in the face of short-run fluctuations in the world market prices of the primary products.

(ii) There is the problem of choice between a higher level of consumption at present and a higher rate of growth in income in the future. Other things being equal, the higher the target rate set for future growth, the greater the sacrifice in the form of a lower rate of increase in consumption at present and/or the longer the period of waiting before the fruits of economic development are available. In so far as a more vigorous pursuit of economic development policies involves increasing present sacrifice or prolonging the waiting period, it tends to intensify rather than ease the subjective problem of discontent and 'the revolution of rising expectations'. The extent to which an underdeveloped country can vary its time-pattern of income and consumption is determined by two limits: the extent to which it can cut down present consumption and mobilize saving; and the extent to which its given institutional and productive framework is capable of absorbing these savings productively. While the operative limit for the overpopulated countries at a later stage of development may be the ability to save, the operative limit for other countries at an earlier stage of development may be the ability to invest productively.

(iii) There is the problem of choice between economic equality and economic growth. Economic equality may be pursued for its own sake, irrespective of its effect on growth. Frequently, where wealth and income are distributed very unequally and where the rich are not making effective use of their income for productive purposes, it may be possible to promote both greater equality and growth by reforms to remove economic inequalities. But frequently also there may be a genuine conflict between economic equality and economic growth. This may operate all the way from the removal of surplus people from land and the consolidation of holdings for the sake of more efficient farming, to the provision of higher rewards to people with higher ability.

(iv) Finally, there is the problem of choice for the mass of people in the underdeveloped countries between having higher material incomes and a faster rate of growth and preserving their traditional social, cultural and religious values and ways of life. Here, the type of psychology attributed to them by Western writers has undergone an amusing change. In the old days, the people of the underdeveloped countries were supposed not to respond to economic incentives and prospects of material improvement. This was the basis of the theory of the backward-bending supply curve of labour and the policy of using negative coercive measures instead of positive economic incentives for increasing the supply of labour to the mines and plantations. Nowadays, the people of the underdeveloped countries are supposed to be pressing forward to raise their material income level at any cost. The new picture seems to be as much a caricature as the old one. Anyone would wish to raise his income if this involved no cost, and the people of the under-developed countries are no exception to this. The real question is how far they are willing to change their ways of life, values and attitudes towards matters such as work, saving or size of family in order to enjoy a higher material level of income.

Market mechanism and economic development

Without attempting to go exhaustively into the complex issues of the relative roles of market forces and state action in economic development, I shall bring together a number of points which have emerged from my analysis.

There is a considerable pessimism among writers on the underdeveloped countries concerning the use of market forces to stimulate rapid economic development. They believe that while the market mechanism can deal with small and piece-meal changes, it is too weak to bring about a large concerted 'big push' necessary to overcome the indivisibilities and break through the interlocking vicious circles. This is paralleled by an equally widespread distrust of the market forces among the governments of the underdeveloped countries. Here, the main objection to the market mechanism arises not from considera-tions of economic growth but from considerations of economic equality and security. It is believed that the free play of market forces will tend to exaggerate the inequalities of income and economic power between the indigenous peoples and the foreign enterprises which operate in their countries. These different beliefs reinforce each other to form a general presumption in favour of greater state action and against the use of the market forces both among the economists who write about the underdeveloped countries and among those who run these countries.

But given the different types of underdeveloped countries and their different stages of development, it is questionable whether this general presumption against the use of the market mechanism is any more appropriate for promoting economic development in all these countries than the general presumption in favour of a laissez-faire policy in the past. Much will depend on the particular circumstances of each type of underdeveloped country.

For instance, we have seen that a large number of under-developed countries, notably in Africa, are still in the early stages of the development of the exchange economy, with the larger part of productive resources still in the subsistence economy. In such a country, even the most planning-minded government would have to start by encouraging the development of an exchange economy as the chief method of mobilizing the resources of the subsistence economy. Development planning requiring fiscal and monetary policies is simply not feasible before the money economy has developed to a certain stage. There is of course no need to wait for the unaided working of the market forces to bring about this development. In the past, even the laissez-faire minded colonial governments encouraged the growth of the money economy, particulary through the provision of better transport and communications.

As we move to the later stages in the development of an underdeveloped country, the factors entering into the appropriate balance between the public sector and the private sector become more complex. For one thing, economic development is not a once-over attempt to increase output, but a continuing long-term process. For instance, a five year development plan has to be judged, not only by its direct measurable addition to output, but also by its indirect long-term effects on the building up or destruction of the institutions which have an effect on the future productive capacity of the country. Thus, in trying to strike a balance between the public and the private sector we should take into account not only their present comparative efficiency but also their different potentialities of improvement in the future. The balanced growth approach is useful in stressing certain complementarities between the state sector, providing the social overhead capital, and the private sector. But it also underplays the fact that this complementarity is possible only in so far as the country has unused resources. Once the bottleneck in a scarce factor such as capital or foreign exchange has developed, then future expansion of the two sectors will become increasingly competitive. Then some choice has to be made between allowing the private sector to expand in relation to the public sector, using the indirect method of harnessing the market forces to stimulate development, and expanding the public sector at the expense of the private sector, relying mainly on the direct method of promoting development.

The unbalanced growth approach illustrates the method of harnessing the market mechanism for economic development. In the short run, the market mechanism deals with a shortage of a particular commodity or factor of production by raising its price sharply enough to cut down demand and equate it to the given supply. In the long run, it deals with a shortage by raising the price of the scarce commodity high enough to induce the increase in its supply. Now, although the price of the scarce commodity rises in both cases, the ways in which it may be raised to solve the short-run and the long-run problems are different. A short sharp rise in the price is effective in cutting down demand, but it may not be the best way of stimulating the long-term supply, and may simply lead to 'windfall' gains which do not affect supply. What is likely to be more effective for stimulating the long-term supply is a somewhat smaller rise in the price, but maintained steadily over a period of time. In contrast to the balanced growth approach which favours a crash programme and a big push forward simultaneously on all fronts, the unbalanced growth approach may be looked upon as a method of applying a smaller but steadier push or pull on certain selected sectors of the economy, which might yield to a concentrated force sustained over a period of time.

It is generally agreed that the state should take a longer term view of gains and losses than private persons. But the state cannot take a longer term view than private persons on all lines of economic activity without forcing on private persons heroic sacrifices of present consumption for the sake of a higher future rate of economic growth. For some underdeveloped countries, there may be little choice but to follow this heroic pattern of forcing economic growth, approaching the 'communist model'. But for other countries which are unwilling or unable to follow this path, and which still have enough elbow room in underdeveloped natural resources to try less heroic methods, the state can best exercise its function of taking the longer-run view and 'sticking its neck out' in particular directions. This means deliberately *distorting* the price and cost differentials and holding on to these distortions (as in the case of an effective protectionist policy or a farm-support programme to increase the food supply) instead of letting the prices and costs be distorted by random imperfections of the market and short-run and speculative factors associated with inflation and balance of payment difficulties. These deep and sustained explorations of particular sectors of the economy by state action may reveal economic opportunities overlooked by the light reconnaissance of private enterprise normally concerned with making quick profits. Further, state action may be used in strengthening the market mechanism of the underdeveloped countries where it is weakest; that is, in the allocation of resources between different periods of time which can be effectively performed only by a fully developed market for capital funds and commodity markets dealing in 'futures'.

Education and investment in human capital

A popular argument for extending the public sector and direct state action for economic development is that there is a shortage of private entrepreneurs in the underdeveloped countries. This overlooks the fact that, in order to have successful economic development by direct state action, the same scarce entrepreneurial qualities are needed in the public sector also, and that there is a general shortage of entrepreneurs and managers in both sectors. The administrative machinery in most underdeveloped countries is notoriously weak, and to extend the public sector is to overburden their civil servants with a horde of new entrepreneurial and managerial functions before they are effectively able to fulfil their basic administrative functions such as the maintenance of law and order, the provision of essential public services and the collection of taxes.

It is now increasingly recognized that many underdeveloped countries may be held back, not so much by a shortage of savings as by a shortage of skills and knowledge resulting in the limited capacity of their organizational framework to absorb capital in productive investment. Thus, attention has shifted from capital to education, from investment in material capital to investment in human capital. This is a great advance on the older approach of trying to mobilize the brawn-power rather than the brain-power of the people of the underdeveloped countries as illustrated by the theory of 'disguised unemployment'. But even the new approach has not fully faced up to the difficult problems of raising the level of skills in the underdeveloped countries.

First, it is too readily assumed that the problem can be solved by breaking the bottlenecks on the supply side. If there are too many lawyers and too few engineers, for example, then it is thought that this can be cured by opening more engineering colleges. This ignores the vital role which salary differentials (combined with prestige and security) play in allocating skilled manpower into different occupations. There are too many lawyers and too few engineers in some underdeveloped countries because lawyers earn more than engineers. The opening of more engineering colleges without upgrading the rewards from engineering will not increase the members of that profession. This is one of the instances where the indirect method of stimulating development through the manipulation of the market mechanism is likely to be very effective. In a moment we shall see the reasons why the overcrowded learned professions of the underdeveloped countries should be so responsive to demand factors.

Secondly, it is too readily assumed that the specific types of skills required for development can be foreseen in advance so that educational expansion can take place by supplying the correct number of 'missing components' of various types which can be neatly fitted into a given framework. This approach works well enough in the earlier stages of educational expansion immediately after political independence, where there are unfilled vacancies and obvious gaps left by the departing expatriates. But just as the expansion of manufacturing industry through import-substitution has a limit, there is a limit to educational expansion through the process of job redistribution. Beyond this point the creation of new jobs to absorb the expanding numbers of graduates from schools and universities becomes more important. Now the rate at which a developing country can absorb the new supply of trained people is basically limited by its general rate of economic growth. But in order to accelerate economic growth, the existing supply of trained people must be capable of providing dynamic leadership: this may take the form of improvements and radical adaptations in the administrative and organizational framework, increasing its capacity to absorb capital for development; or it may take the form of technical innovations, research and new applications of existing knowledge to local problems. In either case, it becomes more important to increase the supply of more qualified administrators, entre- preneurs, and general scientists rather than to increase the specific type of people who can be fitted as missing components into a given framework. It is more difficult to increase the supply of administrators, entrepreneurs and general scientists, since their basic function is to change the economic organiza- tion of the country in more productive directions instead of being fitted into a given framework.

This distinction is also important in assessing the value of foreign technical experts to the developing country. They are most useful where there is a definite niche in the organization of a developing country into which they can be fitted. But once they go beyond the function of being missing components, to try to become dynamic agents of change within the government framework, they are likely to meet with less success. For this, the knowledge of local conditions is more important than just general 'technical know-how', and foreign experts generally do not stay long enough in a country to acquire it. At the other extreme, foreign teachers may be able to perform the very valuable function of transmitting the general scientific methods and approaches to problems.

The last weakness of the 'investment in human capital' approach is that it tends to think too much in terms of applying *material* resources, such as providing more educational build- ings and equipment, to increase human capital. This ignores the fact that in most developing countries the really serious limitation to the formation of new human capital is the meagre initial supply of human capital, in the form of limited numbers of qualified people. The various alternative uses of these very scarce human resources give rise to much the hardest problems of choice: first, between using them in directly productive occupations or in the teaching profession for further capital formation; and second, between various ways of using a given teaching capacity, which leads us to the thorny problems of the educational policy for economic development.

If it is accepted that economic development requires a class of exceptionally able people with high qualifications to provide the dynamic leadership, then the appropriate policy would be to restrict the number of students to that which can be effectively taught with the existing numbers of teachers and to give them intensive training according to their ability. This is the educational equivalent of 'tightening the belt' for those who are not accepted and using 'capital-intensive' techniques in human terms for those who are accepted. But in most developing countries powerful forces are working in the opposite direction. The governments are faced with popular demands for equal educational opportunities, not only between the rich and the poor which do not conflict with selection according to ability, but also between the more gifted and less gifted students. These demands can be met only by spreading the existing teaching capacity so thinly over everyone that it becomes ineffective.

What has happened in many developing countries, particularly in Asia, is that the governments have embarked on 'crash programmes' of educational expansion well beyond the capacity of the limited number of teachers. When these badly taught children finish their secondary school, they can find few opportunities for employment or apprentice training as in the advanced countries. Thus, a much larger proportion seek entry into universities and other institutions of higher education which are in their turn suffering from acute shortage of teaching staff. The general lowering of academic standards which follows tends to lower the efficiency of the graduates employed both in the private and the public sector, and does not promise well for the formation of a dynamic leadership for economic development. What is more tragic, the high quality human resources which could have provided such a leadership remain imperfectly mobilized or wasted through the over-crowding of the educational institutions and the impossibility of giving selective teaching and attention to the more gifted students. This also means that fewer students are qualified for study abroad. In recent years the number of scholarships offered by advanced countries on both sides of the Iron Curtain has outstripped the supply of suitable students from the underdeveloped countries, and this in spite of the vast reservoir of human ability which remains locked within the overcrowded educational systems of these countries.

Whatever the idealistic reasons for which the governments of the developing countries embarked on 'crash' educational programmes, the real driving force behind the popular demand for education on the part of the students and their parents is the desire to obtain good jobs afterwards. The image which inspires them is still that of the educated élite enjoying a standard of living many times higher than the per capita income level of their country. This is in fact the most important way in which 'the revolution of rising expectations' works among the educated classes of the developing countries. Few governments have been able to resist its pressure and follow a more selective and functional educational policy which might promote economic development. Yet few countries can go on absorbing poorly trained university graduates at a faster rate than their general economic growth. Sooner or later, with their present pattern of educational expansion, many developing countries will have to contend with one of the most explosive problems of discontent and frustration: that of graduate unemployment.

M

International aid

At the end of Chapter 6, we saw that the volume of international aid to the underdeveloped countries has steadily risen from around $2 billion a year in 1954 to around $3½ billion a year by 1960.[1] Allowing for the rising population in the receiving countries and for rising prices during the period, this still remains a remarkable development and shows how firmly the general principle that the richer countries should help the poorer countries has now been established in international opinion. Nevertheless, it is still important to recognize that the dilemmas and harsh problems of choice facing many developing countries can be greatly eased by a further expansion in the volume of international aid. It is on this basis that much of the writings on the developing countries has been geared to the purpose of making a persuasive case for increasing aid to them. In this book, I have set myself a different aim—the study of the economics of these countries as an academic discipline. I have done this, not because of a lack of appreciation of the practical importance of increasing aid to those developing countries which can effectively absorb capital. Rather, my aim is based on a deeper appreciation of the fact that, even with generous aid which can ease their situation, the developing countries cannot ultimately escape having to make difficult and painful choices to promote economic development and that it is therefore more important to bring out these choices in their stark outlines than to try to soften their edges by an appeal for more aid.

The fact that generosity does not dispense with the need for

1. For further details, see United Nations Report on *International Economic Assistance to the Less Developed Countries*, New York 1961. The total capital transfers to the developing countries have been estimated at $5·9 billion in 1958 by the GATT Report on *International Trade 1959*.

making difficult choices is true not only for the aid-receiving countries, but also for the aid-giving countries. This may be best illustrated by the problems of choice involved in the allocation of international aid itself. Theoretically, there are at least three possible ways of allocating aid among the underdeveloped countries. (i) One may divide the total available aid equally on a per capita basis; in this case, aid would be distributed too thinly to have much effect. (ii) One may adopt the purely humanitarian principle of poor relief and concentrate aid on the poorest among the underdeveloped countries, irrespective of their capacity to use aid effectively for economic development; in this case, some of the poorest countries may become a permanent burden on the richer countries. (iii) One may select a few developing countries at a more advanced stage of general economic development which seem most capable of absorbing aid for further development and concentrate aid on them, irrespective of their degree of poverty. Having assisted them across the threshold of the 'take-off' into self-sustained growth, and this may take longer than is generally assumed, one may then select the next promising group of countries for similar treatment.

In the light of my analysis stressing the differences between the underdeveloped countries with respect to their general level of development and their capacity to absorb capital, the third method seems to offer the most effective way of using aid to promote economic development—assuming that the aid-giving countries are only concerned with helping the developing countries without wishing to satisfy other economic and political aims. Mr Shonfield, who advocates this method, has suggested three obvious claimants for aid on this principle at the moment—India, Brazil and Mexico.[1] India is a strong case both on account of her extreme poverty and her capacity to absorb aid effectively. Moreover, both India and Brazil seem

1. A. Shonfield, *The Attack on World Poverty*, pp. 61–70.

to have reached a point at which their capacity to absorb capital productively has outstripped their capacity to borrow further on a commercial basis. During the last decade, India has obtained the bulk of the total lending by the World Bank and now with her low ratio of exports to national income and limited possibilities of expanding exports, she can no longer hope to meet the rising burden of debt service payment on further loans.

The way in which international aid has actually been distributed among the developing countries does not follow any of the three possible patterns I have mentioned. There is a considerable variation in the per capita amount of aid received, ranging from $36·30 for Jordan to $0·02 for Yemen during the period 1957–8–1958–9. Nor is there any connection between the degree of poverty of the receiving countries and the per capita amount of aid they receive. In fact during the period 1957–8–1958–9, there seems to be an inverse relation. Thus, the countries with per capita incomes below $100 have received $1·55 of aid per head; the countries with per capita incomes between $100 and $200 have received $2·41 of aid per head; and the countries with per capita incomes above $200 have received $3·65 of aid per head.[1]

It is also worth noting that over 90% of aid is given on a bilateral basis, and the aid-giving countries, although moved by a genuine desire to promote economic development, are also influenced by considerations of real or imaginary national economic and political interests. A greater degree of inter-national co-ordination can reduce the wastes arising from duplication and competition among different aid-giving nations even within the Western group.[2] But the basic weakness seems

1. United Nations Report on *International Economic Assistance to the Less Developed Countries*, pp. 44–5.
2. However, there are also some promising developments in inter-national co-operation in aid giving. Apart from the Colombo Plan, the most interesting development is the Aid-India Consortium made up of a

to arise from a lack of clear thinking about the aims of aid-giving and the inability or unwillingness to make the awkward political and economic choices necessary in directing aid to those countries which are most capable of using it for economic development.

Here the issues have been further confused by some of the advocates for increasing international aid. Instead of clearly stating their altruistic principle that the aim of economic aid should be only to help the developing countries and that the richer countries should be prepared to meet the considerable cost of giving aid without expecting anything in return, they have tried to use persuasive arguments appealing to the national self-interest of aid-giving countries.

One favourite line of persuasion is to say that international aid through tied loans will expand the export markets of the aid-giving countries. Now, as Mr Shonfield has argued,[1] there may be something to be said for tied loans in so far as the aid-giving capacity of some of the richer countries is limited by their balance of payments considerations, but the 'principle of mutual convenience' which he advocates depends on the coincidence that the particular type of commodities which the aid-giving countries can easily spare happen to be those which are most urgently wanted by the aid-receiving countries. It may be true that the scope for this mutually convenient form of aid is larger than it appears at first sight, but sooner or later it will come to a limit, and at this point the aid-giving countries will have to be prepared to put up with inconvenience and cost. Similarly, it is not true to say that aid-giving is 'costless'

number of industrial countries including Japan and also the World Bank and the International Development Association. The Consortium pledged $1052 million of aid to India in August 1963. If we adopt the method of concentrating on a few of the most promising underdeveloped countries, then the Consortium seems an appropriate method of channelling and co-ordinating aid.

1. A. Shonfield, op. cit., Ch. 11.

because it stimulates employment in the aid-giving countries; in so far as these countries have unemployed resources in general they can use them for a number of good purposes at home such as slum clearance and housing, or improved hospitals and roads. The most important form of 'costless' aid-giving is the free gifts of surplus commodities which have been induced by the farm-support programmes in the aid-giving countries, notably the United States. Here, in so far as the extent of the agricultural subsidies is determined by the internal politics of the aid-giving countries, the food surpluses are genuinely costless and serve to reduce the vital food gap of the overpopulated countries like India, although they tend to depress the export trade of rice from Burma and Thailand. But the argument for *increasing* the agricultural subsidies in the aid-giving countries so that they may give more food away to the underdeveloped countries will have to be carefully scrutinized to find out whether the same amount of extra resources applied directly to the agriculture in the under-developed countries might not yield higher returns.

The other favourite line of persuasion is to use the Cold War argument that economic aid to the developing countries is an 'insurance against Communism'. This is not the place to enter into the broader political questions such as how far those overpopulated countries who feel obliged to adopt the heroic method of forced industrialization 'on the communist model' can hope to carry it out within the framework of 'democratic planning' and how far the 'mixed economy' prescribed for this purpose can maintain a political equilibrium, resisting the centrifugal forces pulling it to the extreme right or to the extreme left. But as I have said right at the outset of this book, it is necessary to distinguish the problem of raising the material standard of living from the problem of easing the tensions created by subjective discontent. Economic development generally requires a time-lag before it can yield palpable results, but in the meantime the process of development is likely to create a considerable amount of dislocation and discomfort for the people. In so far as economic aid is properly used to promote economic development rather than to bribe the discontented, it is not likely to be a reliable 'insurance against Communism'.

The danger of trying to use persuasive arguments on the people of the advanced countries to give more aid to the people of the developing countries is that it may mislead not only the former but also the latter. The system of 'tied loans', for example, which under some circumstances may be a helpful way of increasing the total volume of aid to the developing countries, has become increasingly discredited in their eyes. Given the continual befogging of the issues, we cannot blame the people of the developing countries if they sometimes find it hard to distinguish the 'crypto-philanthropists' who hide altruism under the mask of national self-interest from the 'neo-colonialists' whom they suspect of hiding national self-interest under the mask of altruism.

Finally, excessive emphasis on international aid should not distract our attention from one very powerful way in which the richer countries can help the poorer countries; that is, by giving them better opportunities to trade. As we have seen, one path of relief for the thickly populated developing countries is to export labour-intensive manufactured goods such as textiles to the advanced countries where they come into competition with the old established but frequently less efficient industries of the advanced countries. This is where the 'cost' of helping the underdeveloped countries simply by letting the principle of comparative costs take its course may hit the advanced countries in a concentrated way in the declining sectors of their economy. This is likely to arouse more opposition than general propositions to increase aid, and may put the altruism of the advanced countries to a severe test.

Last—and, for many developing countries, towering above other issues—is the problem of stabilizing the prices of their primary exports. Some of them may lose as much or more through a decline in the prices of their exports than they receive in aid. Most of them would prefer a substantial rise in their export earnings to an equivalent amount of aid. There is no practicable means of raising and stabilizing their export prices permanently above the world market trends. But there is undoubtedly a very strong case for more vigorous international co-operation to smooth out the short-run violent price fluctuations, through commodity agreements and buffer stock schemes. These schemes are admittedly not easy to operate and are full of formidable technical problems and problems of reconciling the national self-interests of producers and consumers. But they have also been neglected because they fall between two stools. The problem of financing them is too much of a short-term problem for the World Bank which is concerned with longer-term problems of economic development. But it is too much of a long-term problem, requiring locking up substantial sums for many years, for the International Monetary Fund concerned with the shorter term problems of monetary stability.

Short General Reading List

Argawala, A. N. and Singh, S. P. (eds.), *The Economics of Underdevelopment*, Oxford University Press, Bombay 1958

Bauer, P. T. and Yamey, B. S., *The Economics of Under-developed Countries*, Cambridge Economic Handbooks, London 1957

Cairncross, A. K., *Factors in Economic Development*, Allen and Unwin, London 1962

Frankel, S. H., *The Economic Impact on Underdeveloped Societies*, Blackwell, Oxford 1953

Hazlewood, A. D. (ed.), *The Economics of 'Under-developed' Areas*; An Annotated Reading List, Oxford University Press, 2nd ed., London 1959

Higgins, B. H., *Economic Development*, Norton, New York 1959

Hirschman, A. O., *The Strategy of Economic Development*, Yale University Press, New Haven 1958

Kindleberger, C. P., *Economic Development*, Harvard University Economics Handbook Series, McGraw-Hill, New York 1958

Lewis, W. A., *The Theory of Economic Growth*, Allen and Unwin, London 1959

Meier, G. M. and Baldwin, R. E., *Economic Development*, Wiley, New York 1957

Meier, G. M., *International Trade and Development*, Harper and Row, New York 1963

Morgan, T., Betz, G. W. and Choudhry, N. K., *Readings in Economic Development*, Wadsworth, Belmont, California 1963

Nurkse, R., *Problems of Capital Formation in Underdeveloped Countries*, Blackwell, Oxford 1953

Nurkse, R., *Patterns of Trade and Development*, Wicksell Lectures 1959, Stockholm 1959

Rostow, W. W., *The Stages of Economic Growth*, Cambridge University Press, Cambridge 1960

Sen, A. K., *Choice of Techniques*, Blackwell, Oxford 1960

Shonfield, A., *The Attack on World Poverty*, London 1960

Index